DATA PROTECTION OFFICER

D1479169

COMPUTERS

Johnssen, Filip

Data protection officer

BCS, THE CHARTERED INSTITUTE FOR IT

BCS, The Chartered Institute for IT, is committed to making IT good for society. We use the power of our network to bring about positive, tangible change. We champion the global IT profession and the interests of individuals, engaged in that profession, for the benefit of all.

Exchanging IT expertise and knowledge
The Institute fosters links between experts from industry, academia and business to promote new thinking, education and knowledge sharing.

Supporting practitioners
Through continuing professional development and a series of respected IT qualifications, the Institute seeks to promote professional practice tuned to the demands of business. It provides practical support and information services to its members and volunteer communities around the world.

Setting standards and frameworks
The Institute collaborates with government, industry and relevant bodies to establish good working practices, codes of conduct, skills frameworks and common standards. It also offers a range of consultancy services to employers to help them adopt best practice.

Become a member
Over 70,000 people including students, teachers, professionals and practitioners enjoy the benefits of BCS membership. These include access to an international community, invitations to a roster of local and national events, career development tools and a quarterly thought-leadership magazine. Visit www.bcs.org/membership to find out more.

Further information
BCS, The Chartered Institute for IT,
3 Newbridge Square,
Swindon, SN1 1BY, United Kingdom.
T +44 (0) 1793 417 417
(Monday to Friday, 09:00 to 17:00 UK time)
www.bcs.org/contact
http://shop.bcs.org/

DATA PROTECTION OFFICER

Filip Johnssén and Sofia Edvardsen with John Potts

BCS
The Chartered Institute for IT

Sharp Cookie Advisors is the trade name of Sharp Cookie Advisors AB, org. no. 559019-8700, https://www.sharpcookie.se/en.

Published by BCS Learning & Development Ltd, a wholly owned subsidiary of BCS, The Chartered Institute for IT, 3 Newbridge Square, Swindon, SN1 1BY, UK.
www.bcs.org

Paperback ISBN: 978-1-78017-4365
PDF ISBN: 978-1-78017-4372
ePUB ISBN: 978-1-78017-4389
Kindle ISBN: 978-1-78017-4396

Ebook available

British Cataloguing in Publication Data.
A CIP catalogue record for this book is available at the British Library.

Publisher's acknowledgements
Reviewers: Andy Searle, Jos Creese
Publisher: Ian Borthwick
Commissioning editor: Becky Youé
Production manager: Florence Leroy
Project manager: Hazel Bird
Copy-editor: Hazel Bird
Proofreader: Barbara Eastman
Indexer: Sally Roots
Cover design: Alex Wright
Cover image: istock/prosign
Typeset by Lapiz Digital Services, Chennai, India.

CONTENTS

LIST OF FIGURES AND TABLES

AUTHORS

Filip Johnssén is a Swedish lawyer and currently holds the position of data protection officer at Klarna, Europe's largest fintech bank. He has previously been the group privacy manager at the global manufacturing company Sandvik as well as the data protection officer at the Swedish Security Service. He is also a board member of the Swedish Data Protection Forum. He is a  regular speaker at national and international data protection conferences and a highly appreciated tutor on various privacy courses. He co-hosts one of the largest podcasts completely dedicated to privacy and data protection, *Dataministeriet*.

Sofia Edvardsen is the founding partner of Sharp Cookie Advisors (https://www.sharpcookie.se/en), a technology and digitisation law firm based in Stockholm, Sweden. In her role there she represents sellers and buyers of cloud computing (IaaS, PaaS and SaaS models), software licensing and other technology transactions. She also holds the role of data protection officer for  several global companies as well as start-ups. In addition, she provides services to data protection programmes for healthcare providers and companies in media, marketing, retail and tech. Sofia also leads the Swedish chapter of the International Association of Privacy Professionals (IAPP). In that role, she facilitates the development of privacy-enhancing practices for Swedish industry and the Swedish public sector.

Sofia graduated from the School of Business, Economics and Law at the University of Gothenburg and has a degree from Chalmers University of Technology. She is a certified privacy professional and holds a CIPP/E certification. She has served as in-house legal counsel of a global telecom company, as in-house legal counsel at a technology investment fund, and as a lawyer in the Stockholm and London offices of Baker McKenzie law firm.

TECHNICAL EDITOR

John Potts came to data protection via a somewhat circuitous route. Having had a successful first career with HM Royal Marines, he then became a detective with the UK Metropolitan Police Service. John is currently the operations director at GRCI Law, part of the GRCI group of companies. He heads up a team specialising in outsourced data privacy across all sectors. He is a data protection professional with a wealth of experience gained as the head of information rights and head of information law and security with the UK Metropolitan Police Service. Both roles involved regular contact with the UK regulator, the Information Commissioner's Office. John has worked as the UK police service lead for data protection matters relating to the EU Prüm agreement for the exchange of biometric data across member states and has given evidence to the EU Working Party on Information Exchange and Data Protection (DAPIX) on several occasions. He has worked as a member of several UK National Police Chiefs' Council (NPCC) boards, including the NPCC National GDPR Reform Group, which was responsible for the introduction of the GDPR and the Law Enforcement Directive into the UK police service. He has worked on several high-profile cases regarding information access rights. Since starting with GRCI Law, John has set up and led the specialist Data Breach and DSAR service and is the data protection officer for several of GRCI Law's key clients.

ACKNOWLEDGEMENTS

Writing this book would not have been possible without the understanding and support of my family, especially my wife, Mirva. Thank you for letting me fulfil another dream!

Filip Johnssén

Congratulations to you, the reader, for taking on a stimulating, challenging and rewarding position as a data protection officer! Chances are that you will not often be bored or find mid-career that your chosen path is full of routine work with little impact on your organisation or people's lives. Be the best you can be. Be more than your expertise – more than merely a lawyer, manager or engineer. Above all, be a problem-solver and focus on understanding your organisation's business objectives and how to support senior management, colleagues and customers. If you do, you will be an appreciated and valuable contributor.

I am forever thankful for the intelligence, wit and grace of my loving husband. To my family, I hope that you will grow to be positive and proactive people, rising to meet any challenge you will encounter.

Sofia Edvardsen

We would also like to thank Jos Creese and John Potts for their invaluable input. The book would not be what it is without you. Thank you!

Finally, we would like to thank Ian Borthwick and Becky Youé for their strong support, creative ideas and encouragement to strive on. We are happy to work with editors with such keen understanding and respect for the reader.

Filip Johnssén and Sofia Edvardsen

ABBREVIATIONS

AI	Artificial intelligence
AICPA	American Institute of Certified Public Accountants
APEC	Asia–Pacific Economic Cooperation
BSI	British Standards Institution
CDO	Chief data officer
CEO	Chief executive officer
CFO	Chief financial officer
CIA	Confidentiality, integrity and availability
CICA	Canadian Institute of Chartered Accountants
CIO	Chief information officer
CISO	Chief information security officer
CJEU	Court of Justice of the European Union
CNIL	Commission Nationale de l'Informatique et des Libertés
CPO	Chief privacy officer
DLP	Data loss prevention
DPIA	Data protection impact assessment
DPO	Data protection officer
DSAR	Data subject access request
EDPB	European Data Protection Board
EEA	European Economic Area
ENISA	European Union Agency for Cybersecurity (originally the European Union Agency for Network and Information Security)

ERM	Enterprise risk management
EU	European Union
GAPP	Generally Accepted Privacy Principles
GDPR	General Data Protection Regulation
IAPP	International Association of Privacy Professionals
ICO	Information Commissioner's Office
ISO	International Organization for Standardization
LIA	Legitimate interests assessment
OECD	Organisation for Economic Co-operation and Development
PET	Privacy-enhancing technologies
PII	Personal identifiable information (US terminology)
PPM	Privacy programme management
ROPA	Record of processing activities (also called a data inventory or Article 30 records)
SIEM	Security information and event management
SMART	Specific, measurable, achievable, relevant and time-bound
SOC	Security and operations centre
TNT	Transformation and transition
WP29	Article 29 Working Party

GLOSSARY

This glossary contains short definitions of key terms and concepts as used and defined in the GDPR.

Biometric data: Personal data resulting from specific technical processing relating to the physical, physiological or behavioural characteristics of a natural person, which allow or confirm the unique identification of that natural person, such as facial images, dactyloscopy data or combinations of (online) behavioural data.

Consent: Any freely given, specific, informed and unambiguous indication of the data subject's wishes by which he or she, by a statement or by a clear affirmative action, signifies agreement to the processing of personal data relating to him or her.

Controller: The natural or legal person, public authority, agency or other body which, alone or jointly with others, determines the purposes and means of the processing of personal data; where the purposes and means of such processing are determined by Union or Member State law, the controller or the specific criteria for its nomination may be provided for by Union or Member State law.

Data subject: An identified natural person or a natural person who can be identified, directly or indirectly, in particular by reference to an identifier such as a name, an identification number, location data, an online identifier or to one or more factors specific to the physical, physiological, genetic, mental, economic, cultural or social identity of that natural person.

Data subject access request: A request for access by a data subject pursuant to Article 15 of the GDPR.

Personal data: Any information relating to an identified or identifiable natural person ('data subject'); an identifiable natural person is one who can be identified, directly or indirectly, in particular by reference to an identifier such as a name, an identification number, location data, an online identifier or to one or more factors specific to the physical, physiological, genetic, mental, economic, cultural or social identity of that natural person.

Personal data breach: A security breach leading to the accidental or unlawful destruction, loss, alteration, unauthorized disclosure of, or access to, personal data transmitted, stored or otherwise processed.

Processing: Any operation or set of operations which is performed on personal data or sets of personal data, whether or not by automated means, such as collection, recording, organisation, structuring, storage, adaptation or alteration, retrieval, consultation, use, disclosure by transmission, dissemination or otherwise making available, alignment or combination, restriction, erasure or destruction.

Processor: A natural or legal person, public authority, agency or other body that processes personal data on behalf of the controller.

Profiling: Any form of automated processing of personal data consisting of the use of personal data to evaluate certain personal aspects relating to a natural person, in particular, to analyse or predict aspects concerning that natural person's performance at work, economic situation, health, personal preferences, interests, reliability, behaviour, location or movements.

Pseudonymisation: This means the processing of personal data in such a manner that the personal data can no longer be attributed to a specific data subject without the use of additional information, provided that such additional information is kept separately and is subject to technical and organisational measures to ensure that the personal data are not attributed to an identified or identifiable natural person.

Recipient: A natural or legal person, public authority, agency or another body, to which the personal data are disclosed, whether a third party or not.

Third party: A natural or legal person, public authority, agency or body other than the data subject, controller, processor and persons who, under the direct authority of the controller or processor, are authorised to process personal data.

PREFACE

Being a data protection officer (DPO) involves much more than just knowing the law around data protection, and it is not just about technology and standards. It is a multifaceted role involving many skill sets. Being a DPO is a multitasking exercise like most senior roles. This book will clarify the role of the DPO and give you an overview of practical, tested and proven ways to manage an organisation's data protection practice and compliance. In this book, we have assembled substantial data protection experience around how to build data protection programmes, work with management, and create awareness of privacy and other areas of interest.

Following the introduction of the General Data Protection Regulation (GDPR) on 25 May 2018, many organisations have appointed DPOs, such as yourself, ready to take charge and lead their organisation to new heights. We believe that regardless of whether the role of DPO is a new or existing one for your organisation or yourself, you will need more than knowledge of the GDPR to be successful in your job.

As a DPO, you will serve as a guardian of the values envisaged in the GDPR. You will be positioned right in the middle between the controller, the processor, the data subject and the authorities, taking all stakeholders into consideration in your performance of your tasks.

Having held this position and acted as senior privacy advisers for many years in organisations ranging from international enterprises to fast-growing technical start-ups, we are delighted to be given the chance by BCS, The Chartered

Institute for IT to help you in this role. We hope that this book will provide you with useful information and practical advice to assist you in establishing a rewarding career as a DPO.

AIMS OF THIS BOOK

This book aims to help you as a DPO in your day-to-day work and also as you set up a more long-term strategic data protection programme that can be managed over time. It is not a legal textbook; it is a practitioner's guide based on legal requirements and obligations. It aims to be your companion, helping you to understand the founding principles and essence of your role. It also aspires to act as a reference for the skills and expertise you should have, and to offer insight on how to implement complex legal text in your organisation. By giving concrete examples, we hope to facilitate understanding of the underlying articles and principles of the GDPR and other legal texts. Most of the examples are taken from our own experience and, as such, are real-world lessons from situations we have come across and solved.

While this book is primarily aimed at helping DPOs, anyone with an interest in data protection and/or implementing legal requirements could benefit from reading it. To gain the most from the book, you should have the full text of the GDPR at your disposal.[1] We will only dig deeper into the legal assessment of specific articles, and only outline the more technological side of things, when necessary. It should be emphasised that it is important to distinguish between information security and data protection while reading this book. In Chapter 1 we will discuss how these are connected and dependent on each other.

Many readers may be the first ever DPO in their organisation. Therefore, we will try to describe how to both start a data protection programme and assign responsibilities throughout

---

1   All official versions of the GDPR can be found at https://eur-lex.europa.eu/legal-content/EN/TXT/?uri=celex%3A32016R0679.

the organisation. Keeping on top of developments in the field is essential, whether this means convincing the board that data protection could be a competitive advantage or bridging the gap between IT security and legal. As a DPO, you will likely be involved in designing services and products, defining and reviewing your organisation's security strategy, developing policies and data protection practices, and many, many more things. Most – but not all – of these areas will be covered in this book. Addressing every single aspect of the life of a DPO would make this book far too long and dull. Instead, we have in relevant places included some good-quality references to literature and other resources for your further reading.

1 DATA PROTECTION FUNDAMENTALS

In this chapter, we will examine the basics of data protection as well as the fundamental building blocks of the General Data Protection Regulation (GDPR). More than in any other legal discipline, within data protection it is essential to understand the background and deeper intentions and meanings of the different requirements and obligations outlined in the laws. At least in the European context, the specifications in the data protection laws are based on fundamental human rights. But let us first look at the heritage of modern data protection.

THE ESSENCE AND HISTORY OF DATA PROTECTION

'It's an invasion of my privacy!' has in the past decade been uttered in protest by people in almost every situation imaginable, from those questioning government surveillance to those wishing to make bookings at hotels and restaurants, and of course lately those whose data has been collected by social media platforms and search engines. The diverse use of such a phrase reflects the importance of privacy as a concept. Privacy is part of our lives as human beings and has been around as long as humankind. However, it took until around 1890 for privacy's essential concepts – as we would recognise them today – to be codified and written into law.

In their article written at that time, 'The Right to Privacy' in the *Harvard Law Review*, Samuel Warren and Louis Brandeis argued for a 'right to be let alone'.[1] This came after decades in

---

1   S. D. Warren and L. Brandeis (1890), 'The right to privacy', *Harvard Law Review* 4 (5), 193–220.

which newspapers had been flourishing and journalists had been seeking more and more sensationalist stories to help them sell editions. Modern technological achievements were encouraging this trend, too: the telegraph was followed by the telephone and the modern camera (Kodak) was followed by cinematography. Industrialisation had reached the everyday person in the streets, not just the factories. The cry for privacy grew, as embarrassing and salacious information could travel across a city within hours and to every corner of a country in a few days. It's no coincidence that the phrase 'Extra! Extra! Read all about it!' was coined during this period.

As the 20th century progressed, the situation remained more or less the same. However, with the introduction of more modern technology in general and the internet in particular, the concept of privacy needed an update. In 1980, almost a century after Warren and Brandeis' article, the Organisation for Economic Co-operation and Development (OECD) emphasised the importance of 'protection of privacy and individual liberties with regard to personal data' in its 'Guidelines on the Protection of Privacy and Transborder Flows of Personal Data'.[2] Up until that point, privacy to a large extent had consisted of a right to be left alone, but since then privacy has incorporated the protection of personal information – that is, what we today call 'data protection'. As such, data protection is a sub-category of the right to privacy. In 1981, one year after the OECD adopted its privacy principles, the Council of Europe adopted the Convention for the Protection of Individuals with Regard to Automatic Processing of Personal Data.[3] The convention has since been adopted by 51 parties from countries both within and outside Europe.

Nowadays, threats to privacy and data protection include the development of new technology, poor implementation and use

---

2 'OECD Guidelines on the Protection of Privacy and Transborder Flows of Personal Data' (1980), Organisation for Economic Co-operation and Development, www.oecd.org/internet/ieconomy/ oecdguidelinesontheprotectionofprivacyandtransborderflowsofpersonaldata.htm.

3 'Convention for the Protection of Individuals with Regard to Automatic Processing of Personal Data (CETS 108)' (1981), Council of Europe, https://www.coe.int/en/web/ conventions/full-list/-/conventions/rms/0900001680078b37.

of new technology, uses of personal data in online fraud, and opaque information security in the organisations that guard the data. Examples of negative consequences for individuals include identity theft, discrimination (e.g. where a decision is taken by artificial-intelligence-powered software to exclude a candidate in a recruitment process), and individuals being required to pay higher interest rates on loans due to, in part, their browsing history. Such profiling may also, when poorly implemented, have effects on individuals' political participation. Not only is this intrusive but also individuals usually have no chance to respond to such decisions or attempt to have them changed, due to a lack of transparency. Additionally, in many cases, individuals have little choice about handing over their data to the suppliers of commonplace services and feel compelled to allow their private life to be exposed to some level of risk. Personal data has become a commodity in itself, and as a consequence there is a danger of creating a new type of social inequality between rich and poor. People who can afford it will have privacy – the rest will not.

Up until now, a single individual in many situations has not had the power to challenge or understand these practices or other similar technologies. It was this imbalance that led to the EU's implementation in 2018 of the GDPR, which aims to increase the focus on individuals' rights. Another focus of data protection regulation is the protection of individuals from adverse consequences following the use of their personal data. In essence, data protection's main focus is to protect the use of personal data, ensuring that it is lawful, fair and transparent.

In 2006, Daniel J. Solove made an attempt to identify and understand the different kinds of socially recognised privacy violations in the hope that this would enable courts and policymakers to better balance privacy against countervailing interests.[4] He used existing laws as a source for determining which privacy violations society recognises. However, he went further than just examining the existing privacy practice

---

4   D. J. Solove (2006), 'A taxonomy of privacy', *University of Pennsylvania Law Review*, 154 (3).

as incorporated into law, additionally investigating what society considers worth protecting. He aimed to provide a useful framework for the future development of the law in this area, be it for lawmakers or courts. In the context of the GDPR, we believe that one of his most relevant observations is that 'privacy cannot be understood independently from society'.[5] If you are working in an international environment, even if only within the EU, this is something you must always remember. The GDPR is an attempt to harmonise legislation, but the citizens who live within the countries governed by that legislation have not changed.

Muzamil Riffat has captured this very well, stating:

> A key challenge in any privacy-related discussion is that it is a very subjective phenomenon. A substantial amount of grey area always creeps in whenever attempts are made to define privacy, as there is no universally agreed-upon understanding. The interpretation may vary significantly by country, culture or organization.[6]

Looking at privacy and data protection in this context, a relevant discussion in the light of the GDPR could be whether it is possible to have the same data protection legislation throughout the EU, regardless of the diversity of its countries' histories and social norms. Will a Swede, a Portuguese and a German consider their respective private spheres in the same light? Will they be equally as protective of their personal data? Will they accept the same use of their personal data? In the broader privacy and data protection sense, we could ask ourselves, for example, if the absence of surveillance cameras to preserve privacy is more important than protecting individuals from harassment or assault. Where should we draw the line between privacy/data protection and public safety?[7]

---

5 *Ibid.*, p. 7.

6 M. Riffat (2014), 'Privacy audit: Methodology and related considerations', *ISACA Journal*, 1 January, https://www.isaca.org/resources/isaca-journal/past-issues/2014/privacy-audit-methodology-and-related-considerations.

7 Major aspects of this kind of discussion are not within the scope of the GDPR since public safety and national security are up to each and every member state of the EU.

As a data protection officer (DPO), you should remember that the concepts of privacy and data protection are perceived very differently by different individuals (i.e. the data subjects), and your organisation must take this into account when setting up its data protection practices. The implementation and maintenance of a sustainable data protection programme must also consider this issue. As a DPO, you should emphasise to your organisation how good data protection practices – ones that go beyond legal requirements and meet the expectations of the whole range of people by giving them control over 'their' personal data – can be a competitive advantage.

OECD PRIVACY FRAMEWORK: THE STARTING POINT OF MODERN DATA PROTECTION

Before we proceed further with our investigations into what data protection is today, let us take a closer look at where modern data protection began. As stated above, this can be pinpointed to when the OECD in 1980 adopted its 'Guidelines on the Protection of Privacy and Transborder Flows of Personal Data'. These guidelines are common to almost all data protection legislation in the world, including the GDPR. The guidelines established eight key principles for the protection of personal data:

1. **Collection limitation:** data should be collected lawfully with the individual's permission.

2. **Data quality:** data should be relevant to a particular purpose and be accurate.

3. **Purpose specification:** the purpose of data collection should be stated at the time of the data collection and the use of the data should be limited to this purpose.

4. **Use limitation:** data should not be disclosed or used for different purposes without the permission of the individual.

5. **Security safeguards:** data should be protected by reasonable safeguards.

6. **Openness:** individuals should be informed about the practices and policies of those handling their personal data.

7. **Individual participation:** people should be able to learn about the data that an entity possesses about them and to rectify errors or problems in that data.

8. **Accountability:** the entities that control personal data should be held accountable for enacting these principles.

In 2013 the guidelines were updated[8] and a few additional concepts were introduced, for example:

- **Privacy management programmes:** these programmes serve as the core operational mechanism through which organisations implement privacy protection.

- **Data security breach notification:** this provision covers both notifications to authorities and notifications to individuals affected by a security breach involving personal data.

The influence of the OECD guidelines cannot be exaggerated. Almost all major laws and regulations have used the guidelines as a reference. To mention only a few:

- USA's Cable Communications Policy Act 1984

- Australia's Privacy Act 1988

- New Zealand's Privacy Act 1993

- South Korea's Act on the Protection of Personal Information Managed by Public Agencies 1994

- EU Data Protection Directive 1995

- Asia–Pacific Economic Cooperation (APEC) Privacy Guidelines 2004

- EU General Data Protection Regulation (GDPR) 2018

---

8   'OECD privacy guidelines' (2013), Organisation for Economic Co-operation and Development. www.oecd.org/digital/ieconomy/privacy-guidelines.htm.

Given the major influence of the guidelines, it may be of benefit to use their original eight principles in the implementation of data protection within an international organisation since they are commonly accepted. They are also written less legally than the GDPR (for example), and as such are easier for many people to understand and accept.

One interesting and remarkable detail is that the accountability principle was not implemented in EU data protection law until the GDPR – almost 40 years after its introduction by the OECD.

DATA PROTECTION VS INFORMATION SECURITY

Ever since the introduction of the concept of data protection, much confusion has arisen and much time has been wasted debating the differences and where to draw the line between data protection and information security. In the European context, a good starting point for distinguishing between these disciplines is the definition of data protection in the GDPR. According to the regulation, data protection means 'the protection of natural persons in relation to the processing of personal data'.[9] The basis of this statement is Article 8(1) of the Charter of Fundamental Rights of the European Union and Article 16(1) of the Treaty on the Functioning of the European Union, which provides everyone with the right to the protection of personal data concerning them.

In other parts of the world, what the EU refers to as 'data protection' can be called other things, such as 'data privacy', while 'data protection' at the same time may have other meanings. This discrepancy of terminology sometimes creates confusion in discussions between Europeans and non-Europeans. In the USA, for instance, the protection of personal data (the closest equivalent US terminology to personal data is 'personal identifiable information', or PII) is normally called 'data privacy', whereas 'data protection', at least sometimes, is used more broadly to refer to the prevention of data loss.

---

9 Recital 1 of the GDPR.

7

Now that we know what data protection means, let's have a look at the relationship between data protection and information security.

Information security is only mentioned once in the GDPR. This is because the GDPR does not regulate what an acceptable level of information security is; it merely sets requirements for organisations that use personal data to have adequate processes that ensure that their use is lawful, fair and transparent. Information security is referenced in Article 5(1)(f) of the GDPR, which states that personal data must be processed in a manner that ensures appropriate security of personal data, including protection against unauthorised or unlawful processing and against accidental loss, destruction or damage, using appropriate technical or organisational measures ('integrity and confidentiality'). This refers to what within information security are called the principles of 'confidentiality, integrity and availability' (CIA). As the GDPR consists of many more requirements and obligations, we can conclude that applying information security principles to actual personal data is one important aspect, but far from the whole concept, of data protection. Data protection is much wider in scope and covers all aspects of the *use* of personal data.

A brief explanation of CIA within information security

- **Confidentiality:** access restrictions are in place and data is secured from unauthorised access.
- **Integrity:** keeping data intact, unchanged and accurate over its whole lifecycle.
- **Availability:** information is available to authorised persons when they need it.

That said, and although this book is not about information security per se, the question of creating a good culture of privacy and data protection practice in an organisation should be seen in the wider context of good information governance and in close relation to good security practices.

THE EUROPEAN LEGAL LANDSCAPE

At first glance, the European data protection legislation might seem harmonised and streamlined now that we have the GDPR and several directives in this field. But once you start to scratch the surface, a wide variety of federal laws (at the EU level) and national laws (at the member state level) emerge, making up a spider's web of legislation. To complicate the picture even more, some laws are comprehensive (such as the GDPR) while others relate to specific sectors, such as Directive (EU) 2015/2366 (known as PSD2), relating to payments;[10] directives about data protection in law enforcement;[11] and national legislation around health data and patients' rights. It is important to understand that some processing activities can be governed by one, two or even more laws on both the EU level and the national level. In this chapter, we will first and foremost explore the GDPR, but we will also introduce some of the more significant additional laws that you are likely to come across at one time or another – for example, the ePrivacy Directive.[12]

---

10 'Directive (EU) 2015/2366 of the European Parliament and of the Council of 25 November 2015 on payment services in the internal market, amending Directives 2002/65/EC, 2009/110/EC and 2013/36/EU and Regulation (EU) No 1093/2010, and repealing Directive 2007/64/EC' (2015), European Parliament and European Council, https://eur-lex.europa.eu/legal-content/EN/TXT/?uri=CELEX:32015L2366.

11 'Directive (EU) 2016/680 of the European Parliament and of the Council of 27 April 2016 on the protection of natural persons with regard to the processing of personal data by competent authorities for the purposes of the prevention, investigation, detection or prosecution of criminal offences or the execution of criminal penalties, and on the free movement of such data, and repealing Council Framework Decision 2008/977/JHA' (2016), European Parliament and European Council, https://eur-lex.europa.eu/legal-content/EN/TXT/?uri=CELEX%3A32016L0680.

12 'Directive 2009/136/EC of the European Parliament and of the Council of 25 November 2009 amending Directive 2002/22/EC on universal service and users' rights relating to electronic communications networks and services, Directive 2002/58/EC concerning the processing of personal data and the protection of privacy in the electronic communications sector and Regulation (EC) No 2006/2004 on cooperation between national authorities responsible for the enforcement of consumer protection laws' (2009), European Parliament and European Council, https://eur-lex.europa.eu/legal-content/EN/TXT/?uri=celex%3A32009L0136.

The General Data Protection Regulation (GDPR)

In this section, we will take a closer look at some of the fundamental and more influential stipulations in the GDPR. This is not an exhaustive description of all the articles and their implications, but we have tried to pick out what will most influence your work as a DPO.

Harmonisation and derogations

As we previously stated, one of the most important reasons the GDPR was introduced was the need to harmonise the data protection laws across the EU. But, during the extensive negotiations prior to the GDPR's introduction, it became apparent that the member states were not aligned in all areas. To reach an agreement, extensive possibilities for derogations were incorporated into the GDPR, giving member states the power to override some of its obligations and requirements, such as age restrictions relating to children and how to manage the national public sector. Other sectors were completely excluded from the GDPR, such as crime prevention and national safety.

One area where we have already seen major national legislation since the introduction of the GDPR is processing within employment relationships and business–consumer relationships. Another important aspect left to the member states is whether or not breaches of the GDPR are criminalised. Such differences can have a significant impact on an organisation's risk appetite.

For each market your organisation enters, you will need to explore the national derogations so as to gain a comprehensive picture. Some national derogations must be reported by the member state to the European Commission.[13]

The many possibilities around derogations and the list of areas where the GDPR is not applicable have made Viljar Peep,

---

13 'EU member states notifications to the European Commission under the GDPR' (n.d.), European Commission, https://ec.europa.eu/info/law/law-topic/data-protection/data-protection-eu/eu-countries-gdpr-specific-notifications_en.

director general of the Estonian Data Protection Inspectorate, state: 'We will not see harmonisation in my lifetime.'[14]

Material and territorial scope

In any given data protection situation, the first thing you need to know is whether the GDPR applies to the specific case or not. There are two aspects you need to consider. The first is the type of situation you are facing – specifically, whether it is within the **material scope of the GDPR**. This is about what sort of processing of personal data falls under the regulation. In legal terminology, all processing of personal data that is done 'wholly or partly by automated means' falls within the scope of the regulation. In addition, the scope includes some cases where the processing of personal data, other than by automated means, 'form[s] part of a filing system or is intended to form part of a filing system'.[15]

But what are 'automated means'? The easiest way to think of automated means is that as soon as personal data is in electronic form, the GDPR applies. Thus, a lot of what companies and organisations do will fall under the regulation. Even if it is only one individual's personal data that is resting on a USB device or a file server, without anyone ever accessing it or doing something active with it, it is covered by the regulation and all applicable requirements must be met. It is very important to remember this, since 'processing' is commonly perceived to refer to actively doing things with data, such as amending, analysing or filing. There is no such requirement in the regulation. Data at rest is covered, just like all other actions that may be done with data.

Additionally, what does 'to form part of a filing system' mean exactly? The definition of material scope indicates that some manual handling of personal data is covered. This means that even paper records can be within the scope of the GDPR in some cases. The Court of Justice of the European Union (CJEU)

---

14 Statement made at the Nordic Privacy Arena, Stockholm, 12–13 November 2018.

15 Article 2 of the GDPR.

looked at this issue in the so-called *Jehovah's Witnesses* case.[16] The court concluded, in this quite complex case, that 'it is not necessary that [the handwritten notations from door-to-door preaching] include datasheets, specific lists or other search methods' for them to fall within the material scope of the law. This meant for the Jehovah's Witnesses that their books with notes must be kept in accordance with data protection laws.

The second aspect you need to consider is the **territorial scope of the GDPR**, which regulates the geographical reach of the regulation. The territorial scope is more complicated than the material scope as it depends on various factors. The territorial scope can be divided into two sections: who is processing the personal data and whose data is being processed.

Who is processing the personal data? Article 3(1) of the GDPR stipulates that it applies to 'processing of personal data in the context of the activities of an establishment of a controller or a processor in the Union, regardless of whether the processing takes place in the Union or not'.

The keyword here is 'establishment'. It may sound straight-forward but it is in fact in many circumstances a complicated task to assess where an entity is 'established'. Fortunately, the European Data Protection Board (EDPB) has published a guideline on the territorial scope of the GDPR[17] and the CJEU has thoroughly looked at the concept of establishment through some of its court cases. These cases related to the applicability of the Data Protection Directive, but the EDPB guideline indicates that the interpretations of 'establish-ment' relating to the directive will continue to apply under the GDPR more or less unchanged. You will need to understand the implications of the two most notable cases since they

---

16 *A religious community, such as the Jehovah's Witnesses, is a controller, jointly with its members who engage in preaching, for the processing of personal data carried out by the latter in the context of door-to-door preaching* (2018), Court of Justice of the European Union, https://curia.europa.eu/jcms/upload/docs/application/pdf/2018-07/cp180103en.pdf.

17 *Guidelines 3/2018 on the Territorial Scope of the GDPR (Article 3): Version 2.1* (2018), European Data Protection Board, https://edpb.europa.eu/sites/edpb/files/files/file1/edpb_guidelines_3_2018_territorial_scope_after_public_consultation_en_1.pdf.

will probably affect the application of the GDPR in your organisation, especially if you operate in more than one country.

In the first case, *Weltimmo v NAIH* (commonly known as the 'Weltimmo case'), a Slovakian company, Weltimmo, ran a property advertising website concerning Hungarian properties. The website was in Hungarian and Weltimmo had local sales agents in Hungary and processed the personal data of Hungarian advertisers. In its judgment the CJEU considered Weltimmo to be established in Hungary since it had a website in Hungarian, advertised Hungarian properties, used a local agent, and used a Hungarian postal address and bank account. Consequently, the court concluded that the data protection legislation of one member state (Hungary) could be applied to a company (Weltimmo) despite it being headquartered in another country.[18]

In the second case, *Google Spain SL and Google Inc. v AEPD and Mario Costeja Gonzalez* (commonly known as the 'Google Spain case'), the CJEU declared that Google Inc. (a US-based company) was effectively established in the EU because its search activities, a service offered by Google Inc., were sufficiently linked to the advertising sales generated by its subsidiary, Google Spain.[19]

Even though both cases related to the Data Protection Directive, they are highly relevant as they established that companies in one EU country as well as companies outside the EU could be subject to the Data Protection Directive despite the fact that the directive does not state that it applies outside the EU (unlike the GDPR). Applied to the current legal framework, the cases show that a subsidiary or even a single individual can bring all of its data processing activity within the scope of the GDPR based solely on the establishment ground. Global

---

18 Case C-230/14 *Weltimmo s.r.o. v Nemzeti Adatvédelmi és Információszabadság Hatóság* [2015] ECLI:EU:C:2015:639.

19 Case C-131/12 *Google Spain SL and Google Inc. v Agencia Española de Protección de Datos (AEPD) and Mario Costeja González* [2014] ECLI:EU:C:2014:317.

businesses that want to avoid the GDPR have to show there is no commercial connection between a local operation and a non-EU company. It is important to understand these cases and where to draw the line (i.e. when a company is deemed to be established in another country from its headquarters), both in terms of your own company's operations and processing activities and when your company uses processors. You need to understand whether and how the GDPR applies to different entities in your company group and the companies' processors. This could have implications for how you structure the entities and how data is transferred within the group, as well as for what processors your company chooses to use.

Whose data is being processed? Article 3(2) of the GDPR stipulates that, regardless of who is processing the personal data, it applies to:

> processing of personal data of **data subjects who are in the Union** by a **controller or processor not established in the Union**, where the processing activities are related to

> (a) the offering of goods or services... to such data subjects in the Union; or

> (b) the monitoring of their behaviour as far as their behaviour takes place within the Union.[20]

These premises imply that companies and other organisations, even if they are not present in the EU, must under some circumstances adhere to the GDPR. In legal terminology, this phenomenon is called 'extraterritorial reach'. One example could be a company in Asia that actively targets people within the EU and sells them consumer goods via the internet. Here the Asian company does not need to be established in the EU, as the GDPR will apply anyway. Conversely, the GDPR is probably not applicable if a person within the EU orders goods through a domestic website outside the EU if the retailer doesn't make any attempt to sell to customers within the EU.

---

20 Emphasis added.

Knowing where to draw the line can be very hard, especially in a globalised world where it is often possible to order goods from all around the world and get them shipped to the EU.

> As a rule of thumb, the GDPR is applicable if a company processing personal data is based (incorporated) in the EU, or if a non-EU-based company is targeting or offering goods or services to people within the EU and processing the data of those people.

Main establishment

The term 'establishment' is used in another context in the GDPR too, namely 'main establishment' (Article 4). It is important to understand the difference between whether a controller or processor is **established** in the EU and where its **main establishment** is. The latter is a question for companies with headquarters in one EU member state and subsidiaries in at least one other member state.[21]

For companies operating with subsidiaries in multiple EU member states, it will be of the utmost importance to determine where the main establishment of the company group is, since several obligations will depend on this. For example, it affects which country's data protection authority should be considered the lead supervisory authority.

In the GDPR, the main rule regarding a company's main establishment is that it is 'the place of its central administration in the Union' (Article 4). Normally this is the headquarters or registered head office of a company group. There is one exception to the main rule, and that is if the decisions and power to implement decisions about the company's processing activities are taken in another establishment of the group (i.e. another group company). If that is the case, then this latter company will be considered the main establishment according

---

21 Some guidance can be found in Recital 36 of the GDPR.

to the GDPR, at least as long as it is a company within the EU. When you assess your organisation to determine its main establishment, you should look at objective criteria and only examine where the actual decisions are made, not where the processing is done (see Recital 36 of the GDPR).

For processors, the main establishment is decided slightly differently. The main rule for processors is that the main establishment should be considered to be where the central administration is placed if it is in the EU; alternatively, if the processor does not have any central administration in the EU, the main establishment should be considered to be where the main processing activities take place (i.e. the place of the servers).

DPO's tips

- Determine to what extent your organisation falls within the scope of the GDPR, and, on the basis of this information, how you will manage the fulfilment of the legislation alongside other legal and market requirements. Are you required to appoint a DPO for the GDPR side of the business?

- Encourage your organisation to decide where its main establishment is and consequently what country's authority is the lead supervisory authority. Consider including information about the main establishment in your company's internal data protection policy.

The ePrivacy Directive

Besides the GDPR, the ePrivacy Directive is for many organisations the most important data protection legislation.[22] According

---

22 'Directive 2002/58/EC of the European Parliament and of the Council of 12 July 2002 concerning the processing of personal data and the protection of privacy in the electronic communications sector' (2002), European Parliament and European Council, https://eur-lex.europa.eu/legal-content/EN/TXT/?uri=CELEX%3A020 02L0058-20091219.

to Article 1 of the ePrivacy Directive, it regulates the processing of personal data in the electronic communications sector. It is important to understand that it regulates both the telecommunications industry and electronic communications as such (i.e. every organisation's use of electronic communications regardless of its industry or sector). For example, it regulates how cookies may be used and how direct marketing via email may be deployed. Since it is a directive (and so must be implemented in national member states laws), individual member states may have implemented Article 1 slightly differently; therefore, it is important to investigate the national variations before conducting any direct email marketing. For example, Germany has implemented a so-called double opt-in, which is not seen in any other member state.

Direct marketing via email

The general rule as outlined in the directive is that if an email address is obtained from a customer in the context of the sale of a product or service, this email address may be used for direct marketing of the organisation's own similar products or services. However, customers must be given the opportunity to object, free of charge and in an easy manner. In reality, this means every piece of communication that is sent out must include an unsubscribe link.

Cookies

According to Article 5(3) of the directive, gaining access to information stored in the 'terminal equipment', more commonly known as the device, of a user is only allowed on condition that the user has been provided with clear and comprehensive information, and is offered the right to refuse such processing by the data controller. The right to refuse does not apply if the practice by the organisation is strictly necessary in order to provide a service explicitly requested by the user. Examples of strictly necessary cookies include session cookies used during a purchase flow in order to make sure it is the same customer throughout the purchase.

Tracking technologies and device fingerprinting

The ePrivacy Directive regulates the use of cookies, all access to information stored on a user's device and all placement of information on that device. This means that the same strict rules apply to the practice of collecting different forms of device fingerprinting, including through user agents (i.e. software acting on behalf of users).

Online behavioural data as biometric data

A growing trend in online marketing is to use data from online browsing to build advanced behavioural profiles. In doing so, it is possible to gain insights from and commercialise data of unidentified users. Do not make the mistake of thinking that unidentified online data is not personal data. If it is possible to tie a user to a unique identifier, data often falls within the definition of personal data. The cookie settings and tracking technologies are governed by the ePrivacy Directive while the use of the data is regulated by the GDPR.[23] By using various methodologies to compile and analyse online data, organisations sometimes create a behavioural template. When this is paired with a user's behaviour online (click data, device data, sentiment analysis, how the user moves around or uses an app or webpage, etc.), that user can become identified and separated from a group of unidentified users. Hence, behavioural data may fulfil the criteria for biometric data, requiring additional safeguards and (most often) consent as the legal basis according to the GDPR. (See the section 'Lawfulness of processing (legal basis)' later in this chapter for more information on the legal bases.)

Online identifiers for profiling and identification are mentioned in Recital 30 as follows:

> Natural persons may be associated with online identifiers provided by their devices, applications, tools and protocols, such as internet protocol addresses, cookie identifiers or other identifiers such as radio frequency identification

---

[23] See the excellent *Opinion 5/2019 on the Interplay between the ePrivacy Directive and the GDPR, in Particular Regarding the Competence, Tasks and Powers of Data Protection Authorities* (2019), European Data Protection Board, https://edpb.europa. eu/sites/edpb/files/files/file1/201905_edpb_opinion_eprivacydir_gdpr_interplay_ en_0.pdf.

tags. This may leave traces which, in particular when combined with unique identifiers and other information received by the servers, may be used to create profiles of the natural persons and identify them.

A 'unique identifier' (also called 'biometric data') is defined in Article 4(14) of the GDPR as

personal data resulting from specific technical processing relating to the physical, physiological or behavioural characteristics of a natural person, which allow or confirm the **unique identification** of that natural person, such as facial images or dactyloscopic data.

'Behavioural characteristic' is not defined in the GDPR, but the Article 29 Working Party considers that typical 'behavioural biometric data'

include[s] hand-written signature verification, keystroke analysis, gait analysis, way of walking or moving, patterns indicating some subconscious thinking like telling a lie, etc.[24]

Making good use of online behavioural data may bring many advantages to both organisations and users (personalised services, better adaptation to user behaviour, preferences, etc.). Keep in mind that many of these practices are considered advanced and qualify as high-risk activities in the gist of Article 35 of the GDPR. As such, they will require proper risk assessments and full transparency towards the data subjects.

If your analytics department is working with behavioural or biometric data, you would be wise to prioritise setting up data governance processes to assist them in their work.

Future developments

The European Commission is currently working on turning the ePrivacy Directive into a regulation. The new regulation would

---

[24] Article 29 Working Party (2012), *Opinion 3/2012 on Developments in Biometric Technologies* (201200720/12/EN WP 193), Directorate C of the European Commission, https://ec.europa.eu/justice/article-29/documentation/opinion-recommendation/files/2012/wp193_en.pdf, p. 4.

most likely be broader in scope and include more obligations on organisations. The legislation process started with a proposal from the European Commission in January 2017, but it has been subject to debates and many delays. Revised proposals for the ePrivacy Regulation were rejected by the European Council in November 2019.[25] Any attempt to restart the legislative process must involve revisiting the fundaments of the earlier proposal, which will take additional time.

The interplay between the GDPR and the ePrivacy Directive

The use of cookies falls within the material scopes of both the GDPR and the ePrivacy Directive. In its opinion on behavioural advertising, the Article 29 Working Party (WP29) stated that: 'If as a result of placing and retrieving information through the cookie or similar device, the information collected can be considered personal data then, in addition to Article 5(3), Directive 95/46/EC [i.e. the Data Protection Directive] will also apply.'[26] Case law established in 2018 in the CJEU has confirmed this dual applicability.[27]

The rule is that the placing or reading of cookies must comply with the national legislation implementing Article 5(3) of the ePrivacy Directive. Any subsequent processing must meet the GDPR's requirements on, for example, legal basis in its Article 6. This also means that cookie compliance, in part, is an aspect of a GDPR audit or enforcement action.

---

25 F. Y. Chee (2019), 'EU countries fail to agree on privacy rules governing WhatsApp, Skype', *Reuters*, 22 November, https://www.reuters.com/article/us-eu-eprivacy/eu-countries-fail-to-agree-on-privacy-rules-governing-whatsapp-skype-idUSKBN1XW22P.

26 Article 29 Working Party (2010), *Opinion 2/2010 on Online Behavioural Advertising*, Directorate C of the European Commission, https://ec.europa.eu/justice/article-29/documentation/opinion-recommendation/files/2010/wp171_en.pdf, p. 9.

27 Case C-210/16 *Unabhängiges Landeszentrum für Datenschutz Schleswig-Holstein v Wirtschaftsakademie Schleswig-Holstein GmbH* [2018] ECLI:EU:C:2018:388; Case C-40/17 *Fashion ID GmbH & Co.KG v Verbraucherzentrale NRW eV* [2019] ECLI:EU:C:2019:629.

THE GDPR'S PRINCIPLES FOR THE PROCESSING OF PERSONAL DATA

Just as was the case under the Data Protection Directive, all processing under the GDPR must always be done in accordance with some basic data protection principles. Processing that fails to meet one or more of these principles is inevitably illegal. Most of the principles can be traced back to the early days of modern data protection, especially the OECD's privacy principles in its 1980 guideline.

All other requirements and obligations in the GDPR must be read and interpreted in the light of these principles. Hence, you need to know and understand them to fully comprehend and be able to apply the more specific articles in the GDPR.

Lawfulness, fairness and transparency

The first principle of the GDPR consists of three distinctly different elements. 'Lawfulness' relates to legal compliance with the GDPR and other legislation, 'fairness' relates to best practice and a balanced approach in relation to data subjects, and 'transparency' relates to informing data subjects of the existence of the processing operation and its purposes.

Lawfulness
Lawfulness means that activities must comply with laws and regulations. It should be emphasised that compliance is not restricted to the GDPR. Hence, as a DPO, you must not only know about the GDPR but also have 'expert knowledge of data protection law and practices' (Article 37(5)). Data protection provisions are scattered across many other laws besides the GDPR – for example, employment law, health law, archiving law and marketing law. The proposed use of personal data must, for example, have the appropriate legal basis in Article 6 of the GDPR for the processing to be considered lawful.

Fairness
Fairness means respecting data subjects. For example, this might mean not hiding purposes in complicated language

or not deviating from best practice or common practice in a specific area. Fairness also entails not surprising data subjects, and, if something may be unexpected, being extra-clear about it. Additionally, the fairness principle means that data subjects should be informed if they must provide the personal data that is being requested of them, and told what the consequences could be if they refuse to do so. Within this principle also lies the idea that the controller should make data subjects aware of the risks that specific processing may expose them to (Recital 39). An increasingly important aspect of fairness is that a controller should implement technical and organisational measures that minimise the risk of inaccuracies in personal data. This is especially important in the context of the use of artificial intelligence, which in some cases is very biased and has discriminatory effects.

Transparency

Transparency is the basis for all the rights of data subjects and thus very important for you to monitor. You should be involved in the assessment of all communication with your organisation's customers and employees, and make sure this is done transparently. It is vital that your organisation provides data subjects with all the information that is necessary to enable them to use the rights in the GDPR. The information must be adjusted to the specific circumstances and context of the processing. It is especially important to inform data subjects of any profiling activities and describe in easily understandable language how the profiling is done and the possible consequences of the profiling. How the information is given depends on the context, but it should always be given before the collection of personal data starts.

The most common way of giving data subjects the required information is via a privacy notice.[28] But other solutions are possible as long as they meet the requirements. For example,

---

28 This is not the same thing as a 'privacy policy' or a 'data protection policy'. These are internal documents stating an organisation's privacy or data protection practice. However, there is a common misconception around what notices and policies are. A policy is most often an internal document; however, in American practice, a policy is also the privacy document you provide to your customers with a commercial contract.

during the negotiations prior to the introduction of the GDPR, the European Parliament suggested using icons to improve readability and ease of use of information texts.[29]

Historically, most companies' privacy notices have been written by lawyers using legal language, which can make them difficult for the general public to understand. To overcome this, Article 12 and Recital 58 of the GDPR state that information given to data subjects and communication with them must be easily accessible and easy to understand. These requirements include using clear and plain language.

More about transparency and how to give information to data subjects can be found in Chapter 3.

Purpose limitation

According to the GDPR, all personal data must only be collected for specified, explicit and legitimate purposes. As a consequence, the purpose of gathering personal data must be decided **before** the collection starts. It is not legal to collect first and think of a purpose later. Thus, collecting 'nice-to-have' data is not legal. On the other hand, the GDPR allows for further processing of existing data as long as the new processing is not incompatible with the original purpose. But, even if the new purpose may be compatible, it is also necessary to have a legal basis (in many cases legitimate interest) for this new purpose.

The purpose limitation principle has become more challenging to manage as big data and artificial intelligence have become more and more advanced. One of the founding principles of these fields is to harvest vast amounts of data and try to find new ways of using it over time. With the speed of development,

---

29 'Report on the proposal for a regulation of the European Parliament and of the Council on the protection of individuals with regard to the processing of personal data and on the free movement of such data (General Data Protection Regulation)' (2013), Committee on Civil Liberties, Justice and Home Affairs, European Parliament, https://www.europarl.europa.eu/doceo/document/A-7-2013-0402_EN.html, Amendment 24.

it is very hard to foresee purposes even a year in advance, and practically impossible two or three years from now.

Consequently, before collecting personal data, your organisation must try to imagine future uses of the data and state them in the information given to data subjects, as well as in the record of processing activities (ROPA), according to Article 30.

Data minimisation

Theoretically, adhering to the principle of data minimisation is probably one of the easiest ways for your organisation to stay out of trouble. According to this principle, an organisation must not collect or store data it doesn't need. In other words, it may not collect nice-to-have data, only need-to-have data. Hence, once the purpose of a particular instance of processing has been established, the next step is to determine the minimum amount of data needed to pursue that purpose. All of the collected data must be relevant to the purpose. For example, to deliver goods, a controller probably only needs the name and address of the customer. It doesn't need to know their income or marital status. On the other hand, if the purpose is a credit assessment, the customer's address, income and marital status will probably be highly relevant.

In practice, though, adhering to the principle of data minimisation – and especially regular deletion of data – is much harder than it may seem. This is not least because most organisations must keep data according to legal requirements, such as bookkeeping, besides the data required for their core business purposes. Thus, data collected at the same time point may have different retention periods. Each time it collects data, every organisation should define what data is necessary, the purpose of the data collection and for how long the data should be kept, for example in a purpose and retention matrix.

Adding to this complexity, some of these purposes may be affected by a request to be forgotten, whereas some will not. In most cases, legal requirements to keep data overrule a request to be forgotten, while processing on the legal basis of legitimate interest (e.g. for marketing) in many cases must stop when such a request is received.[30]

For this to work in practice, an organisation should assign data owners to each set of personal data. The data owners should be responsible for registration in the ROPA as well as ensuring that all requirements, including deletion, are met throughout the data lifecycle.

It used to be common practice to collect data for future purposes, even though this was not allowed under the Data Protection Directive, and think of a purpose later. For data-driven organisations, data minimisation will in practice challenge their operating models and even their revenue streams. If a controller has not been able to look into its crystal ball closely enough, it might end up not being able to use data it has collected if a new purpose it wishes to use is not close enough to the original purpose.

Accuracy

The importance of holding correct data cannot be exaggerated. Inaccurate or incorrect data can, when processed, have very negative effects on data subjects and other individuals, such as wrongful decisions and mix-ups. This is why all personal data needs to be accurate and, if necessary, kept up to date. Article 5 of the GDPR stipulates that 'every reasonable step' must be taken to ensure that inaccurate personal data is erased or rectified without delay. These requirements put up a high bar for the controller and imply that it is not allowable to collect data and then just let it rest. Rather, controllers must continually monitor the processes that are in place, keep their data up to date and ascertain correctness. If you in the course of your reviews find data that is incorrect, you should report it to the relevant stakeholder (e.g. the data owner or system owner) and instruct them to correct it.

---

30 Note that marketing in many cases is also regulated by the ePrivacy Directive.

One good solution for obtaining accurate and up-to-date information is to encourage data subjects themselves to keep their details up to date via a user portal. Another way could be to ask for confirmation at every user interaction, or at certain intervals.

Your organisation could also, if necessary, consult external resources, such as public records of addresses and contact details, and check its data against these. This is common practice in many business sectors – for example, debt collection.

The importance of data accuracy in whistleblowing schemes

Whistleblowing schemes are in many industries important means of preventing and finding out about corruption and other forms of non-approved or illegal behaviour, such as sexual harassment. Whistleblowing schemes can be very powerful tools and, as such, the data reported through them must be accurate.

But a challenge with whistleblowing schemes is that they in most cases are based on free-text fields and that anyone can use either the schemes or the fields. The likelihood of mistakes or malpractice is therefore quite high. Data that is clearly of no interest or relevance to a case may be reported – for instance, a whistleblower might report a colleague for fraudulent activities and inadvertently include the names of family members of the colleague in the data. The personal data of the family members should not then be processed further within the case or investigation (unless it is relevant of course).

Another example, and a much harder case to handle, is mischievous allegations – that is, cases where someone just wants to sabotage someone else and therefore blows the whistle maliciously and tells lies. On the one hand, once the allegation has been made, the data relating to it is correct in the sense that it reflects what has been alleged; on the other hand, the content of the allegation itself is wrong (i.e. not accurate). The question then becomes whether the content should be deleted because the allegation was wrong or kept because the data accurately reflects what the whistleblower stated in the allegation. Whether or not the data is deleted, how long it is kept and what aspects of the data are kept must be assessed on a case-by-case basis. If you as a DPO are involved in a data protection impact assessment (DPIA) for a whistleblowing scheme, you must remember to check that such cases are covered.

Storage limitation

Storage limitation is data minimisation for data that has already been collected. Whenever data is no longer necessary for the purpose for which it was collected, it should be deleted or anonymised. As disk space and server space have become cheaper and cheaper, the necessity of continually erasing data to save space has diminished. Just a few years ago, many organisations had to delete data to keep their server costs down. That is no longer the case. At the same time, collecting data has become easier and the amount of data that it is possible to collect increases by the day. Hence, most organisations have collected vast amounts of data without ever thinking about needing to delete it. You should be aware of the presence of any old data. A suggestion is to ask your IT department whether they have any old legacy systems or databases, and conduct a random sample check of the data in those systems. It is not unlikely that you will find some data that should have been deleted.

One major challenge for many organisations when it comes to storage limitation is, as stated above, that some data is processed for more than one purpose, while other data is processed for only one purpose. The consequence is that some data must be deleted altogether, while other data may be kept but only processed for some of the original purposes. To help you manage this, every data point in a system must show both its purpose and its retention period, for example as metadata. For you to be able to monitor whether data is being kept for too long, you must understand the business of your organisation and all of the purposes behind why data is processed.

Storage limitation and deleting data have been the subjects of at least two cases involving the imposition of fines. In the first case, the French data protection authority, the Commission Nationale de l'Informatique et des Libertés (CNIL), imposed a fine on SERGIC, a real estate company. According to the CNIL, SERGIC had stored rental candidates' documents for too long. It should be emphasised that these documents contained sensitive information about the candidates and that SERGIC lacked security measures. The fine of 400,000 euros was based on both aspects of non-compliance.[31] In the second case, the Danish Datatilsynet imposed a fine of 200,850 euros on the furniture company IDdesign for retaining the data of 385,000 customers in its CRM (customer relationship management) system for too long. Datatilsynet also stated that it had considered the company's lack of documentation of retention periods in its assessment.[32] This case emphasises the importance of not only deleting data appropriately but also being able to show that you have made assessments of your purposes and the retention periods for each purpose.

Retention and archiving tables/matrices

As just stated, data should be deleted when it is no longer needed. How long a controller is allowed to keep data is either determined through an assessment based on the purpose or stipulated in law (such as bookkeeping requirements, tax law or anti-money-laundering rules).

In most organisations, some data points (e.g. people's first and last names) are processed for more than one purpose. For

---

31 'Délibération SAN-2019-005' (2019), Commission Nationale de l'Informatique et des Libertés, https://www.legifrance.gouv.fr/cnil/id/CNILTEXT000038552658. See also 'SERGIC: Sanction de 400 000€ pour atteinte à la sécurité des données et non-respect des durées de conservation [SERGIC: Sanction of €400,000 for breach of data security and non-compliance with retention periods]' (2019), Commission Nationale de l'Informatique et des Libertés, 6 June, https://www.cnil.fr/fr/sergic-sanction-de-400-000eu-pour-atteinte-la-securite-des-donnees-et-non-respect-des-durees-de.

32 'Tilsyn med IDdesigns behandling af personoplysninger' (2019), Datatilsynet, https://www.datatilsynet.dk/tilsyn-og-afgoerelser/afgoerelser/2019/jun/tilsyn-med-iddesigns-behandling-af-personoplysninger.

example, firstly, it could be necessary to process a name to provide a service or to deliver a package to a specific address. Secondly, it could also be necessary to process the same name to make a credit risk decision. And thirdly, it will probably also be necessary to process the name for bookkeeping reasons. All of these different purposes have different retention periods. After the specific retention period has ended for a purpose, the name can no longer be used for that specific purpose, but it can continue to be used for the remaining purposes.

As a consequence, almost all organisations should assess all of their purposes and couple these with retention periods and archiving requirements. This will entail defining minimum and maximum periods. Far too often, individuals without legal training think that the GDPR requires them to delete data when in fact there is an obligation to keep it. This can also be true when a data subject submits a request to be forgotten. This right, as already stated, may be overruled by legal obligations to keep personal data, such as bookkeeping laws.

To enable good retention and archiving governance, your organisation should define a corporate policy and issue general schedules with specified periods of retention. The schedule should include data categories, purposes, retention periods and the reasoning behind each retention period – for example, the legal requirement (and the relevant law). The schedule should preferably be created as a matrix or table. Without such a schedule, it is difficult to know what to keep and what to delete. If possible, data should also be tagged (e.g. with metadata) with these periods in your systems right from the point of collection. It may also be necessary for specific departments to set up their own retention schedules.

Table 1.1 shows an example of a retention period matrix.

Integrity and confidentiality

The requirements around integrity and confidentiality in the GDPR resemble classic information security principles, which has led some people to think of data protection as information security. However, as stated above, information security is only a small part

Table 1.1 Retention period matrix with generic examples

Data	Purpose	Retention period	Reason for the retention period
George Smith's name and address	Delivering a package	Until the claims period is over	Legitimate interest
George Smith's name and email	Marketing to customers	The main rule – during the business relationship plus one additional year[33] (or until George opts out)	According to marketing laws
George Smith's name and financial details	Credit decision	Normally around 5 years	According to credit laws
George Smith name	Bookkeeping	Normally 7–10 years	According to bookkeeping laws

of data protection, albeit an important one. Thus, it is important that you at least have a basic knowledge of both information security and IT security. Included in integrity and confidentiality are such things as encryption, firewalls, access management, monitoring, back-up systems, passwords, authentication, information classifications and security awareness.

It is important to take note that Articles 5 and 32 of the GDPR explicitly state that the measures taken should be 'appropriate'

---

33 *Hur länge får personuppgifter bevaras?* [*How Long May Personal Data Be Retained?*] (2015), Swedish Data Protection Authority, https://www.sorenoman.se/documents/datainspektionen/hur-lange-far-personuppgifter-bevaras.pdf, p. 12.

and can be both technical and organisational. This means that the same security is not needed for everything – it depends on what personal data is being held and the purpose of its processing.

Data loss prevention

As malicious intruders have become better and better at what they do, and as data breaches have become more severe, the need to monitor how data flows around has become increasingly important. Data loss prevention (DLP) software is a tool that monitors user behaviour and data flows in a business. Typically, DLP solutions control the endpoint activities, reading and monitoring data streams on corporate networks. They can also monitor data going to different cloud services. DLP solutions can monitor the movement of data, data at rest or both. There are numerous ways in which DLP can be used in data protection management – for example, controlling whether data is sent to unauthorised cloud solutions[34] or whether external emails can be sent with attachments in a specific format. Thus, these tools can help you to find personal data and to assess risks.

However, the use of DLP solutions involves, to some extent, the monitoring of employees. Thus, just as these tools can help in overall data protection management, they may also constitute an intrusion of the privacy of employees. From a data protection perspective, this is a dilemma. To what extent should the legitimate interest of the organisation (to protect its systems, fulfil its obligations under the GDPR, etc.) prevail over the interest of employees' privacy?

A properly implemented DLP solution is a powerful tool to mitigate organisational security and data protection risks, as it monitors the behaviour of internal users that typically can be considered risky (exporting large files, or intense communication at odd times to external recipients, for example).

---

34 Common to most companies is that employees tend to find the easiest solution to a problem – for example, uploading Excel sheets with personal data to a cloud service, either for storage or for analysis purposes – instead of using designated solutions.

The key to solving the dilemma is to perform a proper DPIA early on in the procurement process of the DLP solution.

Accountability

A major change brought about by the GDPR is the explicit introduction of the accountability principle. Organisations are no longer only responsible for being compliant; they must also be able to demonstrate that they are compliant, at any given point in time. The accountability principle entails that both controllers and processors must document all parts of their data protection work (DPIAs, training records, incident logs, decisions about data protection considerations and motivations, etc.) and adopt appropriate internal policies. The implication of the accountability principle is that a more proactive approach to data protection is required.

Even in the absence of any known incidence of non-compliance, the controller or processor must be able to show what it has done to comply with legal requirements and obligations. This will also be needed for requirements and obligations relating to your role as the DPO, such as reporting structure, job description and assigned resources. The information should be included in your plan to monitor that all relevant documentation is in place and up to date.

Accountability can be divided into three stages, based on Recital 74 of the GDPR:

1. Document all measures your organisation has in place to fulfil the applicable requirements and obligations. For example, have a governance document in place indicating how the board of directors delegate their formal responsibility to the organisation.

2. Document the assessments you carry out to show that these measures are appropriate.

3. Document information that demonstrates that the implemented measures are effective (i.e. that, in reality, they have had the anticipated effect).

One way of demonstrating compliance could be adherence to an approved code of conduct or an approved certification mechanism. The idea is that if a controller or processor processes personal data in accordance with pre-accepted codes or mechanisms established by external parties, this implies external approval, either directly or indirectly, by an independent body.

Big picture: Governance

A far too common mistake is for an organisation to have an undocumented or ad hoc governance structure for its privacy and data protection issues. One of the most important compliance actions you can do is to set up a proper governance structure; it is not enough for you to answer questions and address issues as they arise.

You might find yourself as the DPO in an ad hoc organisation, where the various heads of department are allowed to act independently and there is little or no senior management oversight of issues pertaining to data protection risks and conflicting objectives. In such a situation, the DPO is often seen to be the one responsible for 'flagging' any issue and reining in other parts of the organisation.

If you find yourself in this situation, we strongly recommend that you work to put in place a clear governance process and system of organisation. Work hard to gain the board's or CEO's support to form a working group of a few senior management heads who have the mandate to make decisions and accept risks. This kind of governance document is often called an 'internal data protection policy' and sets out the main elements of accountability:

- formal delegation of decision-making from board to compliance committee;
- roles, responsibilities and mandates of the senior management and the DPO;
- data protection strategy;

- the main principles for HR, marketing/sales, tech/ development, business development, analytics/business information and so on.

With a governance structure behind you, you will have the time to act proactively – not merely react to others' questions (or late deadlines or requirements).

DPO's tips

How do you keep track of whether data processing in your organisation adheres to the basic principles? How can your organisation demonstrate this according to the accountability principle?

One good way could be to include these requirements and how they are solved for each type of processing in the ROPA. This is not a requirement but is good practice. In its simplest form, it needs only a yes/no tick-box for each requirement and a sign-off of each answer by the data or system owner.[35]

DATA PROTECTION CONCEPTS

To apply data protection correctly and efficiently, it is essential to fully understand the basic concepts upon which the legal requirements and obligations are built. Starting with what personal data is, we will in this section examine these fundamental concepts so you can better take advantage of the following chapters. Some of the concepts will at first glance seem trivial and easy, but, as you practise your work, you will soon come to learn that they are far from trivial.

---

35 In some organisations it might be a data owner or a process owner.

What is personal data?

'What is personal data?' is the obvious starting point for any discussion about data protection. No other concept in data protection to the same extent relies on context and or demands as much in-depth knowledge about every little detail and angle of processing. On the one hand, even the most fundamental pieces of data about a person may not be personal data, and, on the other hand, even the most generic data may be personal data. All of this is tied to the definition of personal data in Article 4 of the GDPR:

> 'Personal data' means any information relating to an identified or identifiable natural person ('data subject'); an identifiable natural person is one who can be identified, directly or indirectly, in particular by reference to an identifier such as a name, an identification number, location data, an online identifier or to one or more factors specific to the physical, physiological, genetic, mental, economic, cultural or social identity of that natural person.

You will need to differentiate between two distinct situations when deciding whether data is personal data or not: (1) 'normal' filing systems based on unique individuals (e.g. HR systems, medical records or bank accounts) and (2) databases with data that may or may not 'relate' (in the word's most broad interpretation) to an individual (e.g. web traffic databases, geo-tracking technologies or smart meters). Situation 1 is structured based on individuals as 'hangers' from which all other data stems, whereas situation 2 is not. Even though this division is a slight simplification, it can serve as a basis for exploring when data is or is not personal data.

Situation 1
In these circumstances, the starting point is a specific individual who is identified. All data that is subsequently added is considered personal data about this individual – even data that, by itself, would not be considered personal data. For example, the hanger might be 'Filip Johnssén' (a unique name)

and then layer upon layer can be added with data relating to Filip Johnssén. A typical real-world example is your medical records, which are contained in a specific file all about you. All of the data in that file would most likely be considered personal data about you.

Situation 2

Understanding this situation is all about connecting the dots. In this situation, it may be possible to identify a specific individual from data that initially looks like non-personal data. Usually, each single data point does not reveal the person it relates to; however, by adding more and more of these data points, it at some point becomes possible to conclude whom the points refer to. Once a person has been identified, all additional data connected to this person is also considered personal data. One example is geo-location. Most individuals have unique patterns in their movements and whereabouts. For example, you live at a specific address and may travel to work each day at another address. Just these details about your movement could reveal that data is about you. In other circumstances, additional geo-locations might be needed to link the data to you. Maybe you visit your children at the weekends, at another address. The more 'dots' you have, the easier it is to determine the identity of the person at the centre of the data.

This aspect of the definition of personal data is what makes it so hard to truly anonymise personal data.

Distinguishing between situation 1 and situation 2

It is very important to understand the different situations, especially as analytics tools are becoming more and more advanced. You might very well be processing personal data without it being known across your organisation that you are doing so.

We can therefore conclude that the same data can be personal data in one situation and not personal data in another – and, furthermore, the same data point can switch back and forth depending on changes in the context. One example is anonymisation or aggregation. By applying such risk mitigation tools, it will at some point no longer be possible to identify specific individuals. But, be careful when you do this, as there are several techniques that can be used to reverse engineer and identify individuals. A famous, and fortunate, case of un-un-identifying a person was first revealed in 2007 when Interpol managed to un-twirl a picture of a suspected paedophile.[36]

Stakeholders: data subject, controller and processor

Three of the most important stakeholders in data protection are the data subject, the controller and the processor. At least two other stakeholders can be identified and are dealt with elsewhere in this book: society (see 'Legitimate interest' below) and the data protection authorities (see 'Role of supervisory authorities' below).

Data subject
The data subject is the individual, in the GDPR called 'natural person', that data relates to. You become a data subject if you are identified (or could be identified) by data. Under normal circumstances, the notion of the data subject becomes relevant when it is possible (or might be possible) to single out individual persons and identify them from an aggregation of several data points, above all if this identification can be done indirectly – for example, if it is possible to identify and single out one specific person by putting pieces of general information together, such as age, hair colour, eye colour and occupation. At some point, there will only be one person who fits the description, the data subject. See 'Situation 2' above.

All organisations need to understand who their data subjects are since these individuals have rights, outlined in Chapter 3 of the GDPR, that can be enforced against the organisation. Other individuals will in most cases have no rights at all against the organisation.

---

36 M. Nizza (2007), 'Interpol untwirls a suspected pedophile', *The New York Times*, 8 October, https://thelede.blogs.nytimes.com/2007/10/08/interpol-untwirls-a-suspected-pedophile.

Controller, processor and joint controller

The definitions of 'controller' and 'processor' are more or less identical in the Data Protection Directive and the GDPR. At first glance, the definitions may fool you into thinking it is pretty easy to distinguish between the controller and the processor. It is not.

The GDPR's definitions (Article 4) are as follows:

- **Controller:** 'The natural or legal person, public authority, agency or other body which, alone or jointly with others, determines the purposes and means of the processing of personal data; where the purposes and means of such processing are determined by Union or Member State law, the controller or the specific criteria for its nomination may be provided for by Union or Member State law.'

- **Processor:** 'A natural or legal person, public authority, agency or other body which processes personal data on behalf of the controller.'

Differentiating between the roles of controller and processor can be a real challenge in some situations – not least because the same data can be processed by the same organisation as both controller and processor. A typical example of when an organisation is considered a controller is when it processes employee data. A typical example of when an organisation is considered a processor is when it acts as a vendor offering software as a service (SaaS) without knowledge of what data customers are uploading to the service. In other situations, however, you may need to look in depth at how the data is transferred and processed by the parties. The moment a processor does anything with data for its own purposes, regardless of what the purpose is, it has become a controller for that specific processing.

This kind of switch from being a processor to being a controller has far-reaching consequences both for the former processor and for the original controller – normally the customer who shared the data. For example, the controller that shared the data must have a legal basis for doing so on a controller-to-controller footing, and the processor that became a controller must inform all the data subjects according to Articles 12, 13 and 14. Another consequence will be for you as the DPO, since the role differs slightly between organisations that mainly operate as controllers and organisations that mainly operate as processors. Article 39 of the GDPR lists a number of mandatory tasks of the DPO. These may at first look the same, but there is one major difference: a controller's DPO must support the controller in the performance of DPIAs. This requirement is not present for a processor's DPO. That being said, most processors will probably conduct their DPIAs very similarly to how controllers conduct them, to make sure their services will pass the controller's DPIA.

Another difference is likely to be that a processor's DPO will ensure that all technical functionalities are in place — for example, security mechanisms and functionalities to support the controller in case of data subject access requests (DSARs). The reason is that the data will come from the controller and the purposes of the processing will be decided by the controller. Furthermore, a processor's DPO should check that the processor does what the controller tells them to, but the DPO does not need to assess the purposes as such or the retention periods decided by the controller. In contrast, a controller's DPO needs to assess every single purpose and retention period. Along similar lines, the controller's DPO will need to make sure the instructions to the processor cover all necessary aspects of the processing, while the processor's DPO will only assess that the instructions are clear enough and that the processor follows the instructions (still, nevertheless, an important undertaking).

There may also be situations where **joint controllership** is applicable. According to Article 26 of the GDPR, 'where two or more controllers jointly determine the purposes and means of processing, they shall be joint controllers'. A typical situation where organisations are joint controllers is when a parent company operates a master HR or customer database for the use of its subsidies. Another situation is where a market research company retained by a customer decides the means and process of conducting the research for the commissioned report. Where organisations are acting as joint controllers, it is important to have a joint controller agreement.

A beginners' mistake would be to treat all situations as a controller–processor relationship. Start by analysing the situation – in particular, who has the deciding influence over the purpose and means of the processing. Then carefully work out who is the controller and who is the processor, and whether there are parties acting jointly.

Special categories of personal data

Some types of personal data need extra protection since most people consider them especially sensitive. Therefore, Article 9 of the GDPR stipulates that all types of personal data previously defined as 'sensitive' have kept their status but are now called 'special categories' of personal data. To this category, two additional types of data are added under the GDPR: genetic data and biometric data. The full list is as follows:

> Personal data revealing racial or ethnic origin, political opinions, religious or philosophical beliefs, or trade union membership, and the processing of genetic data, biometric data for the purpose of uniquely identifying a natural person, data concerning health or data concerning a natural person's sex life or sexual orientation.

Processing of special categories of personal data is prohibited unless data subjects have given their consent or an exception applies. For example, it is legal to process special categories of personal data without consent for the protection of vital interests of a data subject (e.g. health data in emergencies) or to fulfil a legal obligation of the controller (e.g. rehabilitation within an employment relationship following imprisonment, addiction or illness).

Criminal history

Article 10 of the GDPR places a general prohibition on the processing of information relating to a person's criminal convictions and offences. However, there are two situations in which it is allowable. The first involves the processing of such data on a small scale, for example during recruitment, whereas the second applies when an organisation holds a comprehensive register of criminal convictions. For most organisations, the second case is never relevant as it relates mainly to government bodies holding registers of all criminal verdicts and imprisonments. But it is prudent to be aware that such comprehensive registers must only be kept under the control of official authorities.

In contrast, the first situation is relevant to many, or even most, organisations. According to Article 10, it is allowed when it is either authorised or under the control of an authority, or authorised by national law. Most member states have implemented such authorisations (exceptions) – for example, both Sweden and the UK have made the processing of criminal data possible for certain purposes.

From a legislative perspective, this is an interesting matter since the EU members implemented the corresponding article in the Data Protection Directive in quite diverse ways. Furthermore, the practice of (for example) conducting background checks is handled differently from country to country, and the availability of this type of data is not consistent across the EU. Therefore, if your organisation operates across national borders, it is important to be aware of the possibility of variations in data availability and legacy processes.

Two common examples of when the processing of this type of data may be necessary are 'sanctions list screening' and fraud prevention (or the prevention of money laundering). Some of this processing will be done because it is legally required while some will not. For example, it is sometimes a legal requirement to screen the board members of a company against EU sanctions lists, whereas many companies process this type of data to protect themselves against fraud. Fraud prevention efforts are in some cases a regulatory requirement, but under other circumstances they are only undertaken to protect a company after legitimate interests assessment (see the section 'Legitimate interest' below).

If you need to process criminal data, you will need to consult the applicable national law to learn more about the exceptions. One important aspect of the general prohibition is that a data subject cannot give consent for the processing of personal data that falls under Article 10.

DPO's tips

- Work closely with the right people in your organisation to make sure that your advice is aligned with the realities of the business (e.g. relating to resources, competencies, strategy and constraints).

- Learn why special category data is valuable to your organisation and what purposes it fulfils.

- The use of special category data almost always warrants the performance of a DPIA to identify and assess any data protection risks and mitigation actions.

- Be sure to understand how your organisation may correctly share this type of data with public authorities, justice authorities, and legal entities such as service providers, suppliers or cloud service providers.

- The special category data your organisation holds should be carefully mapped and documented in your ROPA.

- Document the different legal bases your organisation relies on for the use of this data.

- Make an inventory of the different laws and regulations that apply to the use of special categories of personal data (health data, criminal records, etc.)

LAWFULNESS OF PROCESSING (LEGAL BASIS)

Article 5 of the GDPR stipulates that personal data must be processed lawfully, fairly and in a transparent manner. For processing to be lawful, it must be based on one of six legal bases, as stated in Article 6 of the GDPR. Contrary to what is sometimes believed, all of these legal bases are equal in strength, and compliance with them is not a step-by-step exercise starting with consent and ending with legitimate interest – like a ladder. The ladder misconception has led to companies engaging in huge amounts of unnecessary consent-collecting activities. Often, other legal bases are applicable and more appropriate, such as a fulfilment of contractual obligations or legitimate interest. From a business perspective, consent should most likely be the last resort, since data subjects have the irrevocable right to withdraw a given consent at any time.

The following subsections give further details of the six legal bases, which are listed in Article 6 of the GDPR. Articles 7 to 10 provide specifications on how to implement the legal bases in some specific situations, for example to gain consent from children (Article 8) or to process special category data (Article 9).

Consent

The definition of 'consent' in the GDPR is very similar to the definition in the Data Protection Directive, but the GDPR introduced some important clarifications.

In the directive, consent was defined as

> any freely given specific and informed indication of his wishes by which the data subject signifies his agreement to personal data relating to him being processed. (Article 2(h) of the Data Protection Directive)

In the GDPR, consent is defined as

> any freely given, specific, informed and **unambiguous** indication of the data subject's wishes by which he or she,

by a statement or by a clear affirmative action, signifies agreement to the processing of personal data relating to him or her. (Article 4(11) of the GDPR, emphasis added)

Recital 32 of the GDPR states that consent must be a clear affirmative act. This is generally interpreted to mean that implied consent is no longer valid. Furthermore, consent given before the GDPR entered into force is only valid if the already given consent meets the standards of consent introduced by the GDPR.

Another very important clarification is that when data processing has multiple purposes, consent should be given for each one of them. This follows the requirement that the consent must be 'specific'. Thus, it is not possible to bundle purposes together. Equally, if there are multiple purposes, it is not possible to use one without the others.

'Freely given' implies that data subjects must always have the ability not to give consent. If this is not the case, the consent is not valid. For example, if the balance of power between the data subject and the controller is not equal, as in the employment relationship, it is in most cases not possible to obtain valid consent. Additionally, if the provision of a service is conditional on consent to the processing of personal data that is not necessary for the performance of the service as such, the consent is not considered freely given.

Contrary to popular belief, the use of checkboxes is not necessary to collect valid consent. Any statement or other clear affirmative action is enough. Asking data subjects to click a button or toggle a radio button are also possibilities. Thus, checkboxes are only one of many technical solutions for collecting consent.

The burden of proof for a valid consent will always be on the controller. Therefore, it is very important to document all consents gained as well as revoked consents. This is just as important as documenting whether or not two parties have entered into a contract. However, many systems on the

DATA PROTECTION FUNDAMENTALS

market do not facilitate the administration and management of consent. If your organisation relies on consent, it needs to acquire a workable solution for consent management.

In the case of the CNIL versus the adtech vendor Vectaury,[37] the CNIL stated that a party that relies on consent collected by other controllers must clearly be named on the face of the consent statement when the data is originally created. The CNIL also emphasised that plain language should be used when explaining the purposes of the intended processing.

Consent of children

In view of the extra protection most children need, the GDPR introduced specific requirements around children's consent. These requirements apply to what the GDPR calls 'information society services' (Article 8). The general rule is that a child must be 16 years old to give valid consent for these services, but the GDPR allows member states to use another age between 13 and 16 years. Many member states have taken this opportunity and lowered the age.[38]

The requirements around children differ in other areas too. The information a controller gives before collecting consent must be evaluated to make sure it is understandable for younger people. This may relate to what words are used or how the information is given. It is unlikely your privacy notice for adults will be understandable for much younger people. Young people may also be less used to how the general idea of accepting terms and conditions works on the internet: a privacy notice does not need to be accepted as part of the consent process, but nevertheless it is important for all data subjects to understand the importance of reading these documents.

---

37 'Decision MED-2018-042' (2018), Commission Nationale de l'Informatique et des Libertés, https://www.legifrance.gouv.fr/affichCnil.do?oldAction=rechExpCnil&id=CN ILTEXT000037594451&fastReqId=974682228&fastPos=2.

38 13 years: Belgium, Denmark, Finland and Sweden; 14 years: Austria, Italy and Spain; 15 years: Czech Republic and France; 16 years: Ireland, Netherlands, Slovakia and the UK; no specific national regulation: Germany, Hungary and Poland. See Children Online (https://www.twobirds.com/en/in-focus/general-data-protection-regulation/gdpr-tracker/children) for updates.

One of the major questions that arises around services that target children and young people is how to determine whether a specific user has reached the required age to give consent. It may be enough to simply provide a clear statement of the minimum age allowed. The mechanism for authenticating minors' valid consent has yet to be validated by the courts.

Another important point to consider is at what age a child can enter into a valid contract (i.e. accept terms of service). It might be the same age as consent, but it could be another age. However, as stated above, don't collect consent if your legal basis is in fact fulfilment of contractual obligations.

Contractual obligation

The performance of a contract is probably an underused legal basis. Or, at least, it is often the case that controllers mistakenly specify which processing activities are based on a contract and which are based on consent, when in fact all processing is necessary for the performance of the contract and is therefore legal, with the caveat that the data subject must be a direct party of the contract – in other words, the contract must be between the controller and the data subject. The same goes for all processing that is necessary **before** parties enter into a contract. The second scenario is important to remember as it is used in the sales process.

When is contractual obligation valid as a legal basis?

Contractual obligation is valid as a legal basis in two situations:

- when the processing is necessary for the performance of a contract of which the data subject is a party; or

- when the processing is necessary in order to take steps at the request of the data subject prior to entering into a contract.

Two examples of major importance are processing for the performance of a contract of employment and processing for the performance of a contract of purchase. In both cases, if processing is necessary for the controller to perform its obligations under the contract, no additional legal basis is needed. Collecting consent could in these circumstances just be an extra administrative burden, not least because some processing outside the performance of the contract is likely to be able to rest on the legal basis of the legitimate interest of the controller (covered below).

Another example of processing that could, and probably should, be based on the performance of a contract is the various forms of consumer loyalty club. These tend to employ some form of profiling and provide rewards for purchasing behaviour.

The EDPB has provided some examples of when contract is **not** applicable as a legal basis:[39]

- processing for service improvement or developing new functions (better options: legitimate interest or consent);
- processing for fraud prevention (better options: legal obligation or legitimate interest);
- online behavioural advertising (when the processing qualifies as 'profiling' under Article 22 of the GDPR).

For further information on this topic, we recommend reading the clarifying EDPB's guideline on contract as a legal basis in the context of the provision of online services.[40]

Legal obligation

We have previously outlined how most organisations operate within a spider's web of laws and regulations. Compliance

---

39 *Guidelines 2/2019 on the Processing of Personal Data under Article 6(1)(b) GDPR in the Context of the Provision of Online Services to Data Subjects* (2019), European Data Protection Board, https://edpb.europa.eu/sites/edpb/files/consultation/edpb_draft_guidelines-art_6-1-b-final_public_consultation_version_en.pdf.

40 *Ibid.*

with many of these laws requires processing of personal data. For example, in the employment relationship, this includes obligations laid down by law or by collective agreements regarding management, planning and organisation of work, equality and diversity in the workplace, health and safety at work, rights and benefits related to employment, and arrangements relating to termination of the employment relationship.

Other legal obligations may relate to bookkeeping requirements or tax law. There are also some more specific obligations – for example, in finance and international trade, there are legal obligations to screen customers against various sorts of lists, such as EU sanctions lists (as mentioned above).

Legal obligations can also relate to anti-money-laundering legislation or anti-terrorism legislation. This legislation applies to most sectors that handle money in any way – for example, financial services – but also law firms and other organisations that handle client funds.

All processing that is necessary to fulfil these legal obligations is deemed compliant. But, as always, it is important to remember that data kept and processed for these purposes can probably not be used for any other purposes. The basic principles in Article 5 of the GDPR also apply.

Vital interest

Some processing is necessary for the protection of life and health. In some cases, data subjects will not be able to give consent, but it can be anticipated that they would accept the processing since it is necessary to protect their vital interest or those of another natural person. Such processing should be targeted at the interest of one specific individual, as opposed to processing in the public interest (see the next section).

This type of processing could almost be seen as a descendant of what in other legal circumstances is called *negotiorum gestio* (Latin for 'unauthorised administration'). It refers to situations where a person acts in another person's interest and for that person's benefit, but without their consent. Just as with *negotiorum gestio*, processing to protect the vital interest of a data subject can be done under the assumption that the data subject, if able to, would have given their consent.

For example, if you are unconscious, healthcare personnel will in an emergency situation draw blood and test your blood type without waiting for you to come around to provide informed consent. Another example is a chat service for young children in homes with substance abuse where children can get professional help from providers such as Child Helpline International.

Public interest

Just as processing can be done to protect a specific individual's vital interest, processing can also be done in the public interest. Public interest applies when data processing is necessary for the welfare of the general public – for example, humanitarian purposes such as the monitoring of epidemics and their spread, or in humanitarian emergencies, in particular natural disasters. It is worth noting that such processing should always be based on EU or member state law, even though such laws may be general ones, covering several processing operations.

As the concept of public interest has in the past been adopted and misused by totalitarian regimes in Europe, processing personal data for public interest should only apply to processing that is necessary and proportionate in a **democratic society**, to safeguard public security. All these processing activities should be done in accordance with the requirements set out in the Charter of Fundamental Rights of the European Union and the European Convention for the Protection of Human Rights and Fundamental Freedoms – on which the GDPR is ultimately founded.

Legitimate interest

The last (but not the least important) legal basis is processing that is necessary for the legitimate interests of the controller or a third party, except where such interests are overridden by the interests or fundamental rights and freedoms of the data subject (see Article 6(1)(f) of the GDPR). Third parties can here be other data subjects, other companies or society. What this legal basis entails is that the controller should conduct a balancing test. In one hand, they should weigh the interests of the controller (or the third party) and, in the other, they should weigh the interests and rights of the data subject.

The balancing test for legitimate interest is probably the most complex assessment laid out in the GDPR, since controllers must weigh up several different factors. To help with this, WP29, the data protection authorities and data protection organisations have published a variety of guidelines. These commonly recommend performance of a legitimate interests assessment (LIA), which consists of three steps:

1. **Purpose test:** identify your own or a third party's legitimate interest.

2. **Necessity test:** establish whether the processing is necessary to achieve the interest identified in step 1.

3. **Balancing test:** balance the legitimate interest identified in step 1 against the data subjects' interests.

In step 1 your organisation must identify why it would like to process the personal data in question. It could be an interest of its own or an interest of a third party – for example, security or fraud prevention. Neither of these can normally be based on a legal basis other than legitimate interest. Another common purpose of processing undertaken on the basis of legitimate interest is direct marketing (Recital 47). See Recitals 47–59 for guidance on which interests are recognised to be legitimate. Be aware that, in contrast to security and fraud prevention, marketing is regulated by some other laws as well – most notably the ePrivacy Directive, as described earlier in this chapter.

In step 2 your organisation should evaluate the necessity of the processing and whether it would be possible to achieve the interest in a less intrusive way. For example, you may be able to use aggregated information instead of detailed information or use anonymised data in your analysis.

In step 3 the controller (i.e. your organisation) should execute a balancing test to weigh up the interests identified in step 1 against the interest of the data subject(s). This is normally the most complicated part of the LIA. All relevant factors should be considered. One generally accepted methodology is to perform the balancing test in three separate steps:[41]

1. **The nature of the interests:** the following items could be considered.

   - What are the reasonable expectations of the individual – in other words, would an average person expect the data processing to take place?

   - What type of data is involved?

   - Would the controller or processor experience a negative effect if the intended processing could not be carried out?

2. **The impact of the processing:** the controller should consider potential positive and negative impacts on the data subjects resulting from the processing.

   - Is the processing to the benefit of the data subjects?

   - What is the nature of the relationship between the controller/processor and the data subjects?

   - What level of transparency is there in the controller's/processor's privacy information?

   - Are there easy-to-use tools available for data subjects to opt out and restrict unwanted processing?

---

41 Article 29 Working Party (2014), *Opinion 06/2014 on the Notion of Legitimate Interests of the Data Controller under Article 7 of Directive 95/46/EC*, Directorate C of the European Union, https://ec.europa.eu/justice/article-29/documentation/opinion-recommendation/files/2014/wp217_en.pdf, p. 33. Other informative guidance can be found at *Guidance on the Use of Legitimate Interests under the EU General Data Protection Regulation: Version 2.0* (2018), Data Protection Network, https://dpnetwork.org.uk/wp-content/uploads/2018/11/DPN-Guidance-A4-Publication-17111.pdf.

3. **Safeguards that are in place or could be put in place:** the controller should list all the activities taken to mitigate the risks to individuals through the processing and consider these in the assessment. Are they enough or should they be complemented by others?

Balancing all of the above will ultimately result in a residual risk to the individual (the data subject), and the level of this risk can be used to decide whether the processing is allowed or not. It is always up to the controller to demonstrate that its legitimate interest overrides the interest or the fundamental rights and freedoms of the data subject (Recital 69). Furthermore, it must be stressed that the controller should reveal to the data subjects all necessary and relevant information about how it has determined the balance of interests. This information should also be either included or linked in the ROPA.

Examples of common purposes where legitimate interest could be used as the legal basis

- Direct marketing (may apply) (Recital 47)

- Transmitting personal data in shared administrative systems within a group of undertakings (Recital 48)

- Ensuring network and information security (Recital 49)

- Processing for service improvement or developing new functions[42]

- Online behavioural advertising (if not 'profiling' under Article 22 of the GDPR)

---

42 *Guidelines 2/2019 on the Processing of Personal Data under Article 6(1)(b) GDPR in the Context of the Provision of Online Services to Data Subjects* (2019), European Data Protection Board, https://edpb.europa.eu/sites/edpb/files/consultation/ edpb_draft_guidelines-art_6-1-b-final_public_consultation_version_en.pdf.

- Analytics and big data for (certain) customer insights, personalised services and content and so on.[43]
- Fraud prevention (Recital 47)
- Debt collection[44]
- Sourcing of candidates[45]
- Recordings of phone calls to call centres[46]
- Establishment of legal claims[47]

For further reading about legitimate interest, we suggest:

- *Processing Personal Data on the Basis of Legitimate Interests under the GDPR: Practical Cases* (Future of Privacy Forum and Nymity)[48]

---

43 See Article 29 Working Party (2014), *Opinion 06/2014 on the Notion of Legitimate Interests of the Data Controller under Article 7 of Directive 95/46/EC*, Directorate C of the European Union, https://ec.europa.eu/justice/article-29/documentation/opinion-recommendation/files/2014/wp217_en.pdf.

44 'What is the "legitimate interests" basis?' (n.d.), Information Commissioner's Office, https://ico.org.uk/for-organisations/guide-to-data-protection/guide-to-the-general-data-protection-regulation-gdpr/legitimate-interests/what-is-the-legitimate-interests-basis.

45 *Vägledning: Behandling av personuppgifter enligt Dataskyddsförordningen [Guidance: Processing of Personal Data in Accordance with the Data Protection Ordinance]* (2020) Kompetensföretagen, https://www.almega.se/app/uploads/sites/5/2020/02/vagledning-gdpr-2020.pdf.

46 According to a decision by the Danish data protection authority, Datatilsynet, consent is the only valid legal basis for recording the phone calls of consumers. See 'Forbud til TDC om optagelse af telefonsamtaler uden samtykke' ['Prohibition on TDC recording telephone conversations without consent'], 2019, *Datatilsynet*, 8 April, https://www.datatilsynet.dk/tilsyn-og-afgoerelser/afgoerelser/2019/apr/forbud-til-tdc-om-optagelse-af-telefonsamtaler-uden-samtykke.

47 Case C-13/16 *Valsts policijas Rīgas reģiona pārvaldes Kārtības policijas pārvalde v Rīgas pašvaldības SIA 'Rīgas satiksme'* [2017] ECLI:EU:C:2017:336.

48 G. Zanfir-Fortuna and T. Troester-Falk (2018), *Processing Personal Data on the Basis of Legitimate Interests under the GDPR: Practical Cases*, Future of Privacy Forum and Nymity, https://info.nymity.com/hubfs/Landing%20Pages/Nymity%20FPF%20-%20Legitimate%20Interests%20Report/Deciphering_Legitimate_Interests_Under_the_GDPR.pdf?hsCtaTracking=9cf491f2-3ced-4f9c-9ffa-5d73a77a773e%7C7469b2ec-e91c-4887-b5db-68d407654e23.

- *Guidelines on Automated Individual Decision-Making and Profiling for the Purposes of Regulation 2016/679* (Article 29 Working Party)[49]

- *Guidance on the Use of Legitimate Interests under the EU General Data Protection Regulation: Version 2.0* (Data Protection Network)[50]

- 'How do we apply legitimate interests in practice?' (Information Commissioner's Office)[51]

- *Opinion 06/2014 on the Notion of Legitimate Interests of the Data Controller under Article 7 of Directive 95/46/EC* (Article 29 Working Party)[52]

DPO's tips

- It is good practice to use a legal basis other than consent if possible. For example, in many situations it is possible to base your processing on contractual fulfilment.

- Don't be too hesitant to use legitimate interest as the legal basis. As long as you make sure that your organisation has done a proper LIA, legitimate interest is, in fact, a very solid legal basis.

---

49 Article 29 Working Party (2018), *Guidelines on Automated Individual Decision-Making and Profiling for the Purposes of Regulation 2016/679*, Directorate C of the European Commission, http://ec.europa.eu/newsroom/article29/document.cfm?doc_id=49826.

50 *Guidance on the Use of Legitimate Interests under the EU General Data Protection Regulation: Version 2.0* (2018), Data Protection Network, https://dpnetwork.org.uk/wp-content/uploads/2018/11/DPN-Guidance-A4-Publication-17111.pdf.

51 'How do we apply legitimate interests in practice?' (n.d.), Information Commissioner's Office, https://ico.org.uk/for-organisations/guide-to-data-protection/guide-to-the-general-data-protection-regulation-gdpr/legitimate-interests/how-do-we-apply-legitimate-interests-in-practice.

52 Article 29 Working Party (2014), *Opinion 06/2014 on the Notion of Legitimate Interests of the Data Controller under Article 7 of Directive 95/46/EC*, Directorate C of the European Union, https://www.dataprotection.ro/servlet/ViewDocument?id=1086.

ROLE OF SUPERVISORY AUTHORITIES

Article 51 of the GDPR considerably strengthened all EU data protection authorities (appointed as supervisory authorities under the GDPR).[53] Most notable is their ability to uphold the rights and freedoms of data subjects by imposing much stronger sanctions than before. One well-known example is the high fines that supervisory authorities have the power to impose, but other powers can under some circumstances have even more impact on businesses and organisations. This section briefly examines the new role of the supervisory authorities as well as how they collaborate.

To ensure that the authorities can act independently and efficiently in the use of their powers, the GDPR declares that each authority should be provided with the necessary financial and human resources (Recital 120). Furthermore, the authority should in the exercise of its tasks, including using its powers, act completely independently. The members of the authority should also act independently of outside influence and only in accordance with internal instructions.

According to Article 57 of the GDPR, a supervisory authority has a variety of different tasks. Broadly speaking, these can be divided into three main areas:

- monitoring and enforcing the GDPR;
- promoting and creating public awareness;
- advising and helping relevant stakeholders, such as the national parliament, data subjects and data controllers.

In this section, we will only look at the powers of the authorities that are likely to have the most significant impact on controllers and processors.

---

[53] Most member states have more than one data protection authority, but only one of these is a supervisory authority according to the GDPR. See the final section of the chapter for more information.

The powers of the supervisory authorities are outlined in Article 58 of the GDPR. They are divided into three categories: investigative powers, corrective powers, and authorisation and advisory powers.

Investigative powers

The authorities have been given very far-reaching investigative powers to enable them to fulfil their task of monitoring compliance (see Figure 1.1). First of all, they have the power to order a controller or processor to provide all information the authority requires. The authority also has the right to obtain access to the premises of the controller or processor, the on-site equipment used for processing the personal data, all personal data on the equipment, and all other relevant and necessary information.

An investigation may be triggered by a complaint from a data subject, by a news article or by the controller reaching out to the supervisory authority for help with something. It may also be triggered by some new technology the authority sees as leading to high-risk processing. Increasingly, we are seeing that the supervisory authorities are proactive and are performing industry-wide thematic enforcement actions – for example, relating to profiling in a loyalty programme, access restrictions in patient data in healthcare, or the use of consent in adtech. Many authorities publish their enforcement plans for the coming period on their website.

An investigation will normally be called a 'survey enforcement action' and will start with a set of questions to the controller or processor. If the answers are satisfactory, the case will be closed or a decision of correction will be imposed. If the answers are not satisfactory, the next step may be an on-site audit. These steps may also be combined from the beginning. The initial questions are likely to be sent via letter, and the letter may also request an on-site visit. You will be able to tell from the letter what the scope of the audit will be, as the questions and subject of the audit will be specified.

Figure 1.1 Overview of the two main enforcement processes of the supervisory authority

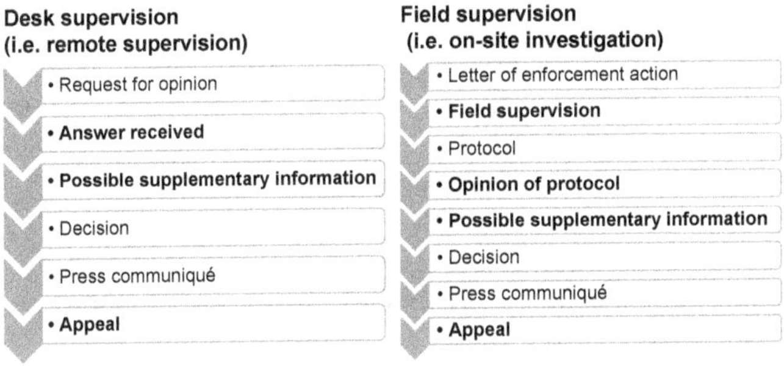

Desk supervision
(i.e. remote supervision)

- Request for opinion
- **Answer received**
- **Possible supplementary information**
- Decision
- Press communiqué
- **Appeal**

Field supervision
(i.e. on-site investigation)

- Letter of enforcement action
- **Field supervision**
- Protocol
- **Opinion of protocol**
- **Possible supplementary information**
- Decision
- Press communiqué
- **Appeal**

Note: bold text indicates tasks performed by the DPO.

As the supervisory authorities' powers of investigation have been strengthened and it is anticipated that on-site audits will become more common, it is wise to prepare a manual setting out your processes and giving details of your team and communication plan, in case of enforcement action. Most important, however, is that the team managing the investigation should be trained and the lines of communication should be open.

During the enforcement action, the authority will ask questions to gauge the existence of any extenuating or aggravating circumstances, such as:

- How did you purchase IT service X?

- How did you ensure all requirements were met?

- Have you been able to make requests relating to the technical design?

- What issues have you raised with the supplier?

- What mitigating actions have you implemented?

- What was your turnover last year according to your latest adopted annual report (for the company subject to the enforcement action and for its parent company)?

You should prepare for the audit thoroughly to enable you to provide clear answers and documentation to support your positions. Much is at stake here, and the formal actions that an authority may take are detailed in the next section. However, organisations may also face commercial liability in contracts, risk being disqualified or sanctioned in publicly procured contracts, experience detrimental effects on their existing insurance cover, and risk negative publicity and loss of customers.

Tips for managing an investigation by a supervisory authority

- Be proactive and present your actions so far concerning the issue at stake – for example:
  - DPIA
  - Mitigating actions implemented
  - Alternatives explored
- Have clear roles and keep everyone involved:
  - Define roles early on
  - The core team will consist of you as the DPO, external legal experts, and business and system experts
- Manage expectations from the very beginning:
  - Set initial expectations and mandate with top management
  - Have regular check-ins with management
- Upon receiving the letter notifying you of enforcement action:
  - Check the scope of the inspection

- Check the mandatory documentation (i.e. the formal information provided by the authority setting out details of the action, such as its scope)

- Identify relevant documentation

- Check whether there are any hints of misunderstandings of your organisation or its business practices

- Field supervision (meaning an enforcement action where the supervisor requires access to the organisation's physical location and hardware/ systems) including review of IT systems:

  - Make it easy

  - Prepare everything

  - Rehearse

  - Summarise

- Receipt of protocol (i.e. a document sent by the authority containing facts they collected during the on-site investigation):

  - Check the accuracy of the supervisory authority's protocol from the field supervision

  - Are there any misunderstandings?

- Preparation of your opinion on the protocol:

  - This is of high importance for the organisation and will affect the outcome of the audit

- Supplementary information:

  - Be proactive

  - Keep an inventory of documents provided

  - Manage any applicable protection processes to ensure confidentiality and avoid sharing privileged information with the authority

Corrective powers

There are three main corrective categories of powers an authority can use:

- issue warnings or reprimands;
- order the controller or processor to take a specific action;
- impose an administrative fine.

It is worth noting that some countries have chosen to include criminal liability for representatives of the organisation, such as the board of directors and CEO. The UK is one of these countries: the Data Protection Act (2018) criminalises alteration of personal data to prevent disclosure or re-identification of de-identified personal data, and it covers directors' liability. In May 2018, the UK enforcement authority stated: 'The ICO will continue its civil and criminal investigations and will seek to pursue individuals and directors, as appropriate and necessary even where companies may no longer be operating.'[54]

Warnings and reprimands

Warnings can be issued **before** processing starts if an authority believes the intended processing is likely to be in breach of the GDPR. Reprimands can be issued **after** processing has started or taken place if the authority considers the organisation to have been in breach of the GDPR. Reprimands are possible only for minor violations and were used during the first year of the GDPR as a show of leniency from the DPAs.

Order to take a specific action

An authority can order a controller or processor to take specific actions, including to honour a data subject's rights. For example, it might order the release of data after a data subject request, or order an organisation to communicate a personal data breach to all affected data subjects.

---

54 Reuters Staff (2018), 'UK data regulator says to keep investigating Cambridge Analytica after closure', *Reuters*, 2 May, https://uk.reuters.com/article/uk-facebook-privacy-britain-data/uk-data-regulator-says-to-keep-investigating-cambridge-analytica-after-closure-idUKKBN1I32UQ?rpc=401&.

Other actions that can be imposed on a controller or processor may have more far-reaching implications. For example, an authority can order a controller or processor to change its processing in a specific way to comply with the GDPR. Such changes could involve reconstructing the infrastructure, changing sub-processors, not processing specific data or deleting all data obtained using the unlawful basis.[55] The order can be accompanied by a deadline. An authority can also order a controller or processor to rectify specific data about a data subject.

The power of the authorities that most organisations should fear the most is the power to order a temporary or definitive limitation or even a ban on processing. This will in many cases call a halt to a business, at least if the processing is business critical. On the plus side is that such a ban should not come as a surprise or straight out of the blue. As stated above in the section on investigative powers, an investigation normally starts with a written communication containing a set of questions.

Administrative sanctions under Article 83
Fines may be combined with any of the other enforcement actions or be imposed as lone sanctions. Article 83 of the GDPR (and the accompanying guidelines) thoroughly outline how fines are calculated and what sorts of infringement of the GDPR are subject to fines.[56]

The largest fine possible is 20 million euros or 4% of the organisation's global annual turnover, whichever is highest. In contrast to what is sometimes stated, there is no fixed limit on the amount. It could be much higher than 20 million euros for companies with a high annual turnover.

---

55 The CNIL ordered the deletion of a large database that contained data that was found to be illegitimate and that had been collected by Vectuary without a legal basis. See 'Décision MED-2018-042' (2018), Commission Nationale de l'Informatique et des Libertés, https://www.legifrance.gouv.fr/cnil/id/CNILTEXT000037594451.

56 Article 29 Working Party (2017), *Guidelines on the Application and Setting of Administrative Fines for the Purposes of the Regulation 2016/679*, Directorate C of the European Commission, https://ec.europa.eu/newsroom/just/document.cfm?doc_id=47889.

This may sound alarming; however, before an authority imposes a fine, it must consider a list of circumstances, and many of these may swing the situation in the organisation's favour. Firstly, the authority will consider the severity of the infringement – for example, the number of affected data subjects, the kind of personal data being processed and the duration of the infringement. Secondly, it will consider what actions the controller or processor has taken to mitigate the negative impact on the data subjects – for example, were adequate safeguards implemented, and was the infringement stopped immediately after discovery? Thirdly, it will consider other circumstances – for example, was the infringement intentional, was it done to gain money and were multiple provisions of the GDPR breached?

Having taken all of the circumstances into consideration, the authority will decide on the best power to use, and fines will only be levied if they are effective, proportionate and dissuasive. For an overview of the GDPR's administrative sanctions, see the GDPR Enforcement Tracker (https://www.enforcementtracker.com).

An interesting aspect of the legislation is that the supervisory authorities will in the future be required to co-ordinate regarding their pending decisions to award administrative sanctions, to ensure a harmonised approach. Initially, we have seen quite a spread in what the different authorities have considered worthy of an administrative sanction, and fines themselves have varied considerably.

Authorisation and advisory powers

Each supervisory authority has within its power to approve codes of conduct and other certification schemes laid out in the GDPR, such as binding corporate rules. It is anticipated that different industries will come up with their own codes of conduct and have them accredited by the authorities. If an organisation later relies on such an accepted code of conduct and processes data in accordance with it, the organisation should be considered to be compliant with the GDPR.

All supervisory authorities also have the power to issue their own guidelines and opinions on data protection matters. They can also advise controllers that seek prior consultation on a specific processing activity (see Chapter 2).

The lead supervisory authority and the one-stop-shop mechanism

One of the big selling points of the GDPR that the legislators used during discussions with representatives of the private sector before the regulation was introduced was the so-called one-stop-shop mechanism. As it was reported, the one-stop-shop mechanism would enable company groups with subsidiaries in multiple EU member states to only deal with one supervisory authority, called the 'lead authority'. If a specific processing activity was 'cleared' by the lead supervisory authority (after consultation with all other relevant authorities in other member states), the processing would be deemed legal in all member states.

The idea of a one-stop shop is manifested in Article 56, where it is stated that the supervisory authority in the country where the company group has its main establishment[57] is deemed competent to act as the lead supervisory authority for cross-border processing. There are some exceptions to this rule and the GDPR contains several provisions that lay out the details of how the supervisory authorities in the member states should co-operate.[58] The main rule for co-operation is that the lead supervisory authority should co-operate with the authorities in EU countries where the controller or processor has an establishment or with affected data subjects. In all cases, the lead supervisory authority must co-operate with a relevant authority in an EU country if a data subject has filed a complaint in that member state.

---

[57] If a company is only present in one country, that is by nature considered to be the location of its main establishment.

[58] These are not outlined in this book but can be found in Chapter 7 (Articles 60–76) of the GDPR.

The co-operation of supervisory authorities is especially important when the lead supervisory authority is about to decide the nature of an enforcement action, since that decision will have a binding effect for the controller or processor in all member states. Therefore, the lead authority must, before such a decision is taken, involve and co-ordinate with all the supervisory authorities concerned in the decision-making process.

From the DPO's perspective, it is probably wise to have a presence in the country of the lead supervisory authority as well as in all other relevant countries. For example, your organisation could appoint privacy champions or give other local employees special training and assignments.

DPO's tips

- Set up a basic team and process for how to manage any contact from the authorities.

- Be proactive. Check whether your organisation is likely to be the focus of a planned enforcement action by reviewing your lead supervisory authority's published enforcement action plan. Synchronise your overall priorities and planned data protection activities with the relevant enforcement objectives of your supervisory authorities.

- Be proactive with the key suppliers you use and ensure you keep track of the relevant documentation on how you have instructed them.

SUMMARY

In this chapter, we have explained the basics of data protection and the GDPR – for example, data protection concepts (such as personal data, data controller and legal basis), GDPR definitions and other legal fundamentals. We have also outlined what a supervisory authority is and what powers it has. All of this is of great importance to understand before we proceed with describing your role as the DPO, and later the various data protection processes in an organisation.

2 THE DATA PROTECTION OFFICER

In this chapter, we look at the objectives, responsibilities, skills and tasks of the data protection officer (DPO) as it is considered in the GDPR and as it is carried out through practice.

The DPO is at best:	The DPO is at worst:
• A risk-savvy diplomat	• A police officer or watchdog
• An adviser and consultant within the organisation	• A whistleblower
• A mediator and negotiator between data subjects' expectations and business needs	• An approver for processing
	• A roadblock or obstacle to processing
• A guardian of personal data	• A decision-maker for the day-to-day management of personal data
• A trust-builder	
• A doer	• A classic IT manager
• A problem-solver	• A classic lawyer or judge
• A jack of many trades (engineering, manager, lawyer, leader, tutor)	• A passive adviser or bystander

INTRODUCTION TO THE ROLE

The role of the DPO, as defined by Articles 37–39 of the General Data Protection Regulation (GDPR), is to:

- advise and inform their organisation of the applicable EU and national regulations, laws and standards;
- advise on data protection impact assessments (DPIAs);
- act as the liaison to the supervisory authority and data subjects.

Assigning a DPO is mandatory under the GDPR for public authorities and private organisations if certain conditions are met. Even for organisations that do not need to appoint a DPO, it may still be advisable to appoint one, or an individual with similar responsibilities.

Origins

In Germany, according to the Federal Data Protection Act 1991, it has been a requirement to appoint a data protection officer since the early 1990s, while the EU as a whole introduced the role of 'personal data protection official' through the adoption of the EU Data Protection Directive in 1995 (see Article 18(2)). The role under the directive was not mandatory, but organisations that appointed such an official had some exceptions concerning other requirements in the directive. According to the directive, the personal data protection official had to keep a register of processing operations and, in an independent manner, monitor their organisation's compliance. In some member states and under some circumstances, the personal data protection official had to report non-compliance of the organisation to the appropriate regulator.[1]

Similar roles are also present in jurisdictions outside the EU; for example, it is mandatory for organisations covered by the

---

1   This obligation is removed with the GDPR.

Health Insurance Portability and Accountability Act 1996 in the USA to appoint a privacy officer.

Purpose

The purpose of the role of the DPO is to provide the leadership, expertise and focus required for organisations to process personal data in accordance with legal requirements and obligations, and in accordance with the expectations of data subjects. As such, the DPO is central in the ability of the organisation to strike a balance between innovation and trust. A successful DPO promotes data protection, collaborative progress and solutions across the organisation, and in this way enables the building of trust between the organisation and its data subjects and enables the organisation to be a trustworthy custodian of personal data.

> The DPO should champion the rights and freedoms of data subjects, while being an enabler of risk management and business innovation.

Legal mandate and liability

First and foremost, it is important to state that the DPO is not responsible or accountable for the compliance of the organisation or personally liable in cases of non-compliance. This will always rest with the organisation as such, regardless of whether the organisation is acting as a controller or a processor.

It is the DPO's responsibility to perform the mandatory tasks stipulated in the GDPR (see the section 'DPO responsibilities' below) under the relevant circumstances. In their execution of these duties, the DPO has the right to access all personal data that the organisation holds and all of its processing operations, and the organisation must make sure the DPO is involved, properly and in a timely manner, in all issues that relate to the protection of personal data (see Articles 38(1) and 38(2) of the GDPR). The DPO may not be dismissed or penalised for performing the mandatory tasks.

When performing their tasks, the DPO is bound by confidentiality enshrined in the GDPR (see Article 38(5)). This is an important aspect since the controller or processor must answer any question by the regulator and disclose information to the regulator upon request. The same is not true for the DPO (i.e. the regulator cannot force the DPO to reveal information).

WHAT MAKES AN EFFECTIVE DPO?

Even though the role of the DPO is defined in the GDPR, it can vary considerably from organisation to organisation based on what each organisation requires in terms of data management and privacy. A common feature is that the role consists of many tasks and combined perspectives. One day the DPO might conduct training and awareness campaigns, the next day they might conduct internal investigations about data protection practice, and yet another day they might attend a conference with DPOs from other organisations in the same business sector to build consensus around market practices. This demands multitasking abilities, great social skills, and the ability to create and uphold trust in the organisation.

An effective DPO must be able to use their knowledge to understand how legal requirements and obligations affect the business. An effective DPO must also be a skilled tightrope walker, constantly balancing being proactive (by providing advice on practical solutions, training and guidance) with being reactive (by monitoring and evaluating actual data protection practices in the organisation).

The aim should always be to support the continuation of business as usual without creating additional layers of unnecessary administration. In most cases, the most efficient way to operationalise data protection without adding too much complexity or administration is to implement the GDPR's data protection principles in the existing business processes, and simultaneously to keep track of issues as they arise and find support in preventing and resolving issues with colleagues at the local level.

Competencies, skills and education

The GDPR sets out specific requirements for the DPO's competencies and skill set. All of these can either be fulfilled by the DPO themselves as a single person or by a team working for the DPO. This is true for internal DPOs as well as for external DPOs engaged via a service contract.

Legal expertise
According to Article 37(5) of the GDPR, a DPO must be appointed on the basis of 'professional qualities and, in particular, expert knowledge of data protection law and practices'. Recital 97 further clarifies that the DPO's knowledge should be proportionate to the complexity of the processing and the protection that is required. For example, where a data processing activity is particularly complex, or where a large amount of special category data is involved, the DPO may need a higher level of expertise. The same is true if the organisation systematically transfers personal data outside the EU, as this is also considered to be complex.

The requirement is formulated in a way that indicates that a DPO needs to have expert knowledge of national and European data protection laws and practices in addition to an in-depth understanding of the GDPR (Article 37). This means that pure textbook knowledge of the GDPR is not enough. It is vital to know the practicalities of implementing various controls and processes. In the case of a public authority or body, the DPO should also know the administrative rules that apply to the organisation. This signifies that an experienced technology and privacy lawyer could be a good fit for the DPO role. Whether or not the DPO must be a lawyer is not stipulated in the GDPR, but it will probably help to have studied law and learned legal ways of thinking and methodology, especially for organisations working in highly regulated business sectors, such as banks or hospitals. But it must be stressed that the GDPR does not require the DPO to have a legal background. In fact, other backgrounds may be a better fit for some organisations – for example, if the processing of personal data is not part of the business as such.

The higher the risk for the data subjects, the stronger the DPO's legal knowledge needs to be since the DPO is likely to need to conduct advanced legal analysis and collaborate with the supervisory authorities.

As stated above, according to the GDPR, the DPO should not only know the law itself but also the practice of the law. The DPO must, therefore, have knowledge of case law, precedents and how the law has been and could be interpreted by authorities and courts.

Furthermore, as the DPO should monitor compliance with the GDPR and provide advice where requested as regards DPIAs, it follows that the DPO must know **all** aspects of the regulation, including how to implement the requirement for the controller to take appropriate technical and organisational measures to ensure the protection of personal data. Therefore, the DPO should have knowledge of information security basics, International Organization for Standardization (ISO) standards, the concept of privacy by design (also called data protection by design) and so on. This is essential since complying with each aspect of the GDPR is likely to require one or more of these standards or frameworks (further information on relevant frameworks, standards and tools is presented in Chapter 6).

Note that according to Article 38(2) of the GDPR, the DPO must be provided with the resources necessary to maintain their expert knowledge. This may be done by setting aside a budget for education or for courses in engineering, law and project management, along with fees for data protection conferences.

Leadership

To be an effective DPO, you must garner the interest and commitment of other key personnel in the organisation where you act. As any person who holds a senior position knows, to earn support and commitment to your cause, you must appear credible and show that you hold the solution and can find synergies with ongoing projects.

Have a strategy for how to create a more detailed data protection strategy once you are on board. Start defining your goal, vision and strategy as early as possible in the recruitment process or when you are negotiating the service contract. Be clear what type of DPO you are (where do you place yourself on the proactive–reactive scale?), and understand your strengths (business centred, technology savvy, strong project leadership skills, etc.) and weaknesses (limited leadership experience, limited experience in a particular technical field, etc.). Early on, help management to articulate what ambitions they have set for the role of DPO in the organisation and how important sustainable management of personal data is to them.

The DPO reports to the highest level of management in the organisation. In most organisations this means the chief legal officer, the chief executive officer (CEO), the chief financial officer (CFO) or directly to the board. The DPO's focus will be different if they work for a mature industry leader where most processes work well compared with an organisation that has immature processes or limited experience focusing on data protection. It is reasonable to assume that your leadership will be tested more thoroughly if you are expected to create and implement new processes across the organisation, rather than just upholding business as usual.

Often you become a leader if and when the organisation acknowledges you as its leader. Trust is earned by being able to set clear goals and articulate expectations on a department level as well as on individual levels. Find allies in the organisation, starting with the CEO, HR manager, chief information officer (CIO), chief information security officer (CISO), chief marketing officer and chief digital officer. Help to define data protection actions that they can implement, measure and report in their respective processes and objectives.

Technical expertise

Data protection has three main controls that offer ways to address and mitigate data protection risks:

- **Technical controls:** the knowledge to build in controls and build around obstacles.

- **Legal controls:** the ability to establish protection from risks in contracts, terms and so on.

- **Organisational controls:** the ability to educate people on how to act responsibly and set up sustainable processes.

As an effective leader, you will need to understand the problems that exist and devise concrete steps to resolve them. Hence, you will not be an efficient DPO who recommends effective solutions to data protection challenges if you do not have more than a basic knowledge of the technical environment. Areas to develop your skills include software development, cloud and server environments, network assets and business analytics. Specialised knowledge is often required in common technology controls such as access management, anonymisation techniques, encryption and logs.

Business knowledge

All the qualities listed above are important, but the most important quality for a DPO is an understanding of the organisation and its processing, and the ability to learn and be attentive to senior management's drivers and objectives regarding how the organisation views data protection and your role. For the DPO to be and stay relevant to the business and not obstruct or impede its operations, they must understand and serve the business. After all, it is the business that decides whether a risk is acceptable or not, which is the meaning of the 'risk-based' approach championed by the GDPR. The most efficient way to stay on top of matters in your organisation is to be relevant to its managers.

Thus, your most important challenge will be to make data protection contribute to the business' goals and convince the whole organisation about why data protection will create value. Think about how data protection and your role could together act as a facilitator and enabler rather than an extra layer of requirements or constraints. If you do not succeed in this, it is very likely you will be seen as an obstacle; soon, no one will come to you and people will instead circumvent you. Sometimes, or even quite often, you will be challenged and questioned. It is at these times that your diplomatic and pedagogical skills will be an invaluable asset.

DPO's tips

Try to never say 'no' and instead give an alternative solution. Make it a habit to say 'yes, **and**...'. Before you provide advice, make sure you understand the problem the business is trying to solve and all stakeholders' angles. And be humble – you may know data protection, but not everyone does. If you adhere to this mindset, you will be successful and add value to the business.

Continued education

As data protection laws and technologies evolve rapidly, DPOs and their staff must have up-to-date knowledge of the relevant fields so that they can carry out their tasks effectively. There has been a proliferation of professional privacy and security certifications, and it is likely that these will be an appropriate means of providing continuing education to you as the DPO and your staff.

As a DPO you should continually develop yourself and your skill set. You are required to have considerable professional qualities and experience and, in particular, expert knowledge of data protection law and practices. These high expectations apply throughout your tenure as a DPO. Thus, you must continue to follow both relevant legislative developments and case law. The possibilities for continued education – provided by private companies but also by universities and special interest organisations – continue to grow. You should probably also attend relevant conferences. Sometimes conferences are packaged together with one or two days of training or workshops. In Appendix 3, we have listed a few conferences that we regularly attend that we think you would benefit from greatly.

Many courses are combined with a test and provide certification. By adding such certifications to your CV, you will evidence the currency of your skills and knowledge. Furthermore, it's always a good idea to broaden your knowledge base and add new skills to complement your existing ones. For example, if you have a legal background, it is probably a good idea to take some courses in information security to start with. On the other hand, if you come from an information security background, it is probably a good idea to deepen your knowledge of the law.

DPO's tips

- Read and understand relevant guidelines from data protection authorities – for example, the French Commission Nationale de l'Informatique et des Libertés (CNIL),[2] the Italian standardisation body (UNI)[3] and the Spanish DPA Agencia Espanola de Protección de Datos (AEPD).[4]

---

2   See *CNIL Certification Scheme of DPO Skills and Knowledge* (n.d.), Commission Nationale de l'Informatique et des Libertés, https://www.cnil.fr/sites/default/files/atoms/files/cnil_certification-scheme-dpo-skills-and-knowledge.pdf.

3   *UNI 11697:2017: Unregulated Professional Activities – Professional Profiles Related to Processing and Protection of Personal Data – Knowledge, Skill and Competence Requirements* (2017), Ente Italiano di Normazione (available through https://www.uni.com on payment of a fee).

4   *Esquema de certificación de delegados de protección de datos de la Agencia Española de Protección de Datos (Esquema AEPD-DPD) [Certification Scheme for Data Protection Delegates of the Spanish Data Protection Agency (Scheme AEPD-DPD)]* (2019), Agencia Española de Protección de Datos, https://www.aepd.es/sites/default/files/2020-07/esquema-aepd-dpd.pdf.

- If your organisation conducts processing in or is affected by the UK, you will need to consult the guidelines of the Information Commissioner's Office (ICO).

- Read and understand the opinions on DPOs issued by the Article 29 Working Party (WP29)[5] and its predecessors, the European Data Protection Board[6] and the European Data Protection Supervisor.[7]

ORGANISATION

As we saw in the previous section, the specifics of the DPO role itself are quite clearly defined in the GDPR. In contrast, the DPO's organisation is described at a high level and in general terms. In this section, we will try to add some clarity to what the GDPR's stipulations could mean for your organisation – for example, in terms of where the DPO role sits in the organisation, conflicts of interest and reporting lines.

Where should the DPO be positioned?

The controller or processor should consider whether the DPO should be a staff member (internal DPO) or fulfil the tasks based on a service contract (external DPO). The most suitable solution depends on the organisation and its current staff members (as also acknowledged by the WP29).[8]

---

5 Article 29 Working Party (2017), *Guidelines on Data Protection Officers ('DPOs')*, Directorate C of the European Commission, https://ec.europa.eu/newsroom/document.cfm?doc_id=44100.

6 'GDPR: Guidelines, recommendations, best practices' (2020), European Data Protection Board, https://edpb.europa.eu/our-work-tools/general-guidance/gdpr-guidelines-recommendations-best-practices_en.

7 'Guidelines' (2020), European Data Protection Supervisor, https://edps.europa.eu/data-protection/our-work/our-work-by-type/guidelines_en.

8 Article 29 Working Party (2017), *Guidelines on Data Protection Officers ('DPOs')*, Directorate C of the European Commission, https://ec.europa.eu/newsroom/document.cfm?doc_id=44100.

In many organisations, the DPO sits within the legal function or the compliance function. It may also be a role without specific organisational allegiance. It is important that the DPO's integrity and independence are preserved; therefore, it is unlikely to be suitable for the DPO to be subordinate to an operational manager such as sales, marketing, IT, IT security or product.

An external DPO is more likely to interact with the general counsel, the CISO or the CFO. In terms of reporting, the external DPO will report to the same role or function as an internal DPO (see the section 'Reporting' below). Furthermore, if an external organisation is serving as the DPO, it is wise to assign a single individual as the lead contact.

The CFO is a suitable representative of the senior management since it is in the CFO's role to apply a long-term perspective to the advancement of the organisation, to manage financial risk and to report to the board on the organisation's performance. An added benefit of the DPO reporting to the CFO is that the CFO most often is part of the board of directors and has a close relationship with the organisation's owners and/or stakeholders. The GDPR requires controllers and processors to interact with the DPO on the highest management level, which is more easily accomplished if the CFO (or general counsel in some organisations) takes part in regular data protection compliance committee meetings with the DPO and all others with a role to play regarding data protection in the organisation. The DPO should be positioned in such a way that they can be involved in the communication flow for activities that are particularly important, such as:

- data breach incidents;
- product development and change processes (the DPO may support risk assessments and DPIAs);
- interactions and communication with data subjects;
- interactions with supervisory authorities;

- interactions with insurance companies in the case of cyber insurance;
- interactions with the organisation's accountants in view of the potential for financial risk.

Independence and conflict of interest

Two of the fundamental tasks of the DPO are to monitor compliance and advise the organisation (including the executive management) regarding data protection requirements and obligations. The independence of the DPO is very important in retaining the trust of all stakeholders, internal as well as external; it is emphasised in Recital 97 of the GDPR that the DPO 'should be in a position to perform their duties and tasks in an independent manner'. To safeguard this, the regulation stipulates that the controller or processor should ensure that the DPO does not receive any instructions regarding the exercise of their regulated tasks. Another way to make sure the DPO is independent is by stipulating a direct reporting line to the highest management level (i.e. to prevent managers at a lower level from 'washing' the DPO's reports) and to ensure that the senior management is aware of the DPO's advice and recommendations.

The independence of the DPO only concerns the DPO's regulated tasks. Thus, the DPO can receive instructions from the organisation for other tasks. However, these instructions may not be made in such a way that they obstruct the DPO from performing the mandatory tasks. How this works in reality is highly dependent on the personal qualities of the DPO and the attitude of the employer. The DPO needs both integrity and a high level of professional ethics. From the outset of your assignment, you should discuss with the organisation how such situations should be dealt with – for example, who should you turn to if you end up in a situation of conflict or your manager gives instructions that could violate your independence?

Another key aspect of upholding trust is the absence of conflicts of interest. This is especially important if a DPO also has other tasks or functions. The other tasks or functions entrusted to the DPO should not be such that they give rise to conflicts of interests or even the suspicion of a conflict of interest.

A decision made by the Bavarian State Commissioner for Data Protection (BayLDA) in October 2016 provides an example relating to a conflict of interest. The BayLDA issued a fine to an organisation for appointing as a DPO an employee who also held the position of IT manager. According to the BayLDA, a DPO cannot fulfil their tasks while also having significant operational responsibility for data processing activities, since this will represent a conflict of interest.[9] According to the WP29, other roles that probably constitute a conflict of interest are senior management positions, such as chief operating officer, CFO, chief medical officer, head of the marketing department, head of human resources or head of IT.

Furthermore, according to a decision by the Belgian Data Protection Authority, a DPO may not have the power to decide that personal data should be deleted, since that would also constitute a conflict of interest.[10] However, a DPO may advise deleting specific personal data.

To safeguard the DPO's independence, it is advised that an internal DPO should have the budget and ability to retain their own legal advice in case they have an alternative opinion to that of the organisation.

Reporting

A DPO should 'directly report to the highest management level of the controller or the processor' (Article 38(3) of the

---

9 *Pressemitteilung: Datenschutzbeauftragter darf keinen Interessenkonflikten unterliegen* [Press Release: Data Protection Officer Must Not Be Subject to Conflicts of Interest] (2016), Bayerisches Landesamt für Datenschutzaufsicht, https://www.lda. bayern.de/media/pm2016_08.pdf.

10 *Objet: Rapport d'inspection relatif à la responsabilité des fuites de données et la position du délégué à la protection des données* [Subject: Inspection Report on Liability for Data Leaks and the Position of the Data Protection Officer] (2020), Autorité de Protection des Données, https://www.autoriteprotectiondonnees.be/publications/decision-quant-au-fond-n-18-2020.pdf.

GDPR). This means that the DPO will be interacting with senior management regularly. If your organisation has a mature data protection function with steering committees, operational committees, and various task forces with defined reporting cycles and/or audit committees, it would be a good idea to join these.

Many organisations do not have a particular function around data protection or compliance. A starting point could be to establish a compliance committee that convenes regularly (such as every other month) and provides sign-off on risk decisions and mitigating actions. The highest management could be represented by the CFO, complemented by the central business positions of the organisation (typically head of sales, chief technology officer and sometimes the head of HR), a privacy liaison and you as the DPO.

You will need to have regular check-ins with senior management to gain their sign-off on processes and risk decisions on topics as wide as vendor management, data breach incident reporting, whether to accept or refrain from a particular instance of processing after a DPIA analysis, how to manage inquiries from supervisory authorities, weighing the data protection risks in a new product under development, and various corrective measures. You can receive such sign-off via your internal hierarchy or (for example) via a compliance committee that convenes regularly and has various task forces (data breach incidents, DPIA task force, etc.).

As mentioned above in the section on leadership skills, a key to success will be the ability to see the bigger picture and uncover the business implications of data protection issues. Check your mandate before you act. Make sure you have a plan that spans the whole organisation, with clear goals and expectations. Be as proactive or reactive as the organisation wishes and needs you to be. Your work and value to senior management are about so much more than the annual or occasional written report – they will often be about how you can simplify matters and guide others (e.g. sales, product and HR) while upholding the speed of daily operations.

Reports that outline gaps without suggesting actionable solutions will probably not be of much value and, in the long run, will lead to trust in you as the DPO being eroded. Hence, we would advise you to focus on processes, in particular if you are the most senior or the sole DPO in your organisation. Try to focus on establishing or improving a few key processes. Perhaps it is the data breach process that could be simplified, or is it time to implement some key metrics?

As when giving any advice, be to the point and accurate. Make sure you have sign-off from the appropriate operational units on facts and are aligned with management's strategy before you present and/or send a report to management. This way, you will ensure your reports are relevant and accurate, and managers will not feel passed over.

If possible, try to report your overall compliance assessment (your compliance audit) before the end of each budget cycle so that the organisation can use the information in its budget planning. If you report after budgeting is closed, there is a risk necessary actions will either be postponed or interfere with planned operational developments, as budgets need to be allocated from these to compliance actions.

Resources and support

As with most roles in a company, budgeting will be a key aspect of your planning and execution of tasks. According to the GDPR, the controller or processor must provide the resources necessary for the DPO to carry out their mandatory tasks (Article 38(2)). This gives rise to some questions: can the DPO require any amount of resources? And can the organisation set the budget for the DPO?

As might be expected, there is little guidance in the actual legal texts regarding budgeting. However, in reality the DPO, or compliance function, will be included in the normal budgeting process and must defend their costs. That being said, if the DPO has a clear, detailed plan for their budget, it will probably be hard for the organisation not to accept the budget.

It is argued that the DPO should have their own resources for the appointment of external consultants in case the DPO has an opinion that deviates from that of the organisation. The GDPR clearly sets out that the DPO is independent and, as such, the DPO should be able to get support and present their view to the organisation, unfiltered by potential internal deliberations. In most cases, the DPO has that ability.

The budget depends on the organisation, but also on how integral data protection compliance is to the core service offerings of the organisation. For example, it is likely that a supplier of cloud services will spend more on data protection than a general consultancy firm or retail shop.

Keep in mind that many projects that will require your expertise and support will pertain to various departments, such as IT, HR, sales and business development. Risk assessments of IT development and participating in data breach mitigation should be included in IT's budget. The DPO's budget should not be the only budget that allows the organisation to carry out its activities in a compliant manner. The first line of defence with regard to data protection is the daily operations in the organisation and these actions should be budgeted as part of the relevant functions' undertakings.

To get the budget or resources you need, a good starting point is to define a target operating model that is in line with the organisation's general operating model, and then prepare a delivery plan. This should be presented to the executive so you can get their approval or at least buy-in. From this point, you should narrow down the areas of expenditure in more detail, prepare a budget and work it into the organisation's approval cycle. For each stage, you should prepare how you will defend your costs in case of objections. You should also anticipate how you could amend your plan if the budget is not approved or is reduced.

The organisation must also support the DPO by allowing them to have access to personal data and data processing operations if necessary. This is to ensure that the DPO can monitor the organisation's actual compliance with legal requirements and internal procedures.

The organisation must support the DPO by:

- giving them the resources necessary to carry out their mandatory tasks;
- giving access to the relevant personal data and processing operations, and allocating the resources necessary to maintain their expert knowledge.

An organisation that does not honour the obligation to provide the DPO with necessary resources and support is at risk of being fined under Article 83(4)(a) of the GDPR at a rate of up to 2% of its worldwide annual turnover.

Start-ups in the strictly regulated fintech and e-health sectors should take steps early on in their funding rounds to secure the relevant resources to train their DPO and staff members. In many cases, it is important to educate investors to make them aware of the necessity of initial and ongoing data protection training for DPOs and staff members so that the investors do not reject such items outright when they consider the financial models presented by start-ups during funding rounds.

Concerning budget and resources, these should not only cover training and the salary of the DPO but also such things as compliance technology and tools (see Chapter 6), IT resources, staffing resources, and access to external legal, technical and consultancy advisers. In large organisations, it may be unrealistic to expect a single DPO to be able to deliver all the DPO's tasks. In practice, DPOs will need to have sufficient resources in terms of access to staff or appropriate teams to ensure that they can discharge all their tasks effectively. For example, DPOs will need access to staff to respond to and deal expeditiously and effectively with internal and external queries, complaints and requests for the exercise of data subjects' rights. As another example, global DPOs will need access to local staff members or external legal counsel who have up-to-date knowledge of the national data protection laws and practices.

Proper and timely DPO involvement

For the DPO to be effective, it is vital for them to be involved in all data protection issues 'properly and in a timely manner' (Article 38 of the GDPR). This is the only way the DPO can work proactively and make sure the organisation thinks of data protection by design and by default when designing new products or services. It is the organisation that is accountable for involving the DPO, not the other way around. The DPO should not be forced to run around and chase down new initiatives.

In practice, this means that the DPO should have the opportunity to give feedback and advice on established processes, risk acceptance levels and priorities. It is not feasible for the DPO to involve themselves directly in any tasks. In this book, direct involvement of the DPO is viewed as a process of escalation, where the organisation wishes to develop strategy, change course in a significant way, or deviate from strategy and risk acceptance levels.

However, in practice, individual employees may forget to involve the DPO. It could therefore be good practice to consider data protection and invite the DPO to be a stakeholder in any forum that approves new products and services.

Furthermore, the organisation should include the DPO as a stakeholder in all relevant internal procedures that could directly or indirectly relate to the processing of personal data. For example, internal project teams may be required to subject their initiatives to a data protection pre-screening process to assist them in evaluating whether data protection issues are relevant and then move on to a full DPIA if needed. Another procedure where the DPO should be involved is procurement. The DPO should have the opportunity to align the procurement processes with applicable data protection rules and apply those rules according to the level of ambition of the organisation.

Related roles and dependencies

As previously described, the role of the DPO can vary between organisations. Consequently, other roles in the organisation may have similar or overlapping responsibilities. In this section, we will explain some of these roles.

Chief privacy officer (CPO)

From a European perspective, the chief privacy officer (CPO) is a rare phenomenon, while many organisations in the USA have a CPO but not a DPO. Even though the DPO role was introduced in Europe more than 20 years ago, it did not receive much attention in the USA until the introduction of the GDPR. The CPO is normally at senior level and does not provide a day-to-day support function to the business. Rather, the CPO's role is to make strategic decisions and set the overall direction of the business. It can most often be found in large company groups with a core business that includes the processing of personal data. For example, Facebook, IBM and the US Department of Homeland Security have appointed CPOs.

One of the major differences is that a CPO will, in contrast to a DPO, make business decisions concerning the data protection practice of the organisation.

Chief information officer (CIO)

As with all titles without a commonly accepted definition, the role of the CIO can vary. The role has changed over time and is sometimes referred to as 'chief technology officer'. Common to all CIOs is that they are the highest-ranking executive dealing with IT. As such, the digital transformation of the organisation is their main task, and they carry it out by setting the long-term strategy and introducing specific initiatives (e.g. deciding to adopt cloud solutions). As such, the CIO is a good liaison point for the DPO.

Chief data officer (CDO)

In 2015, Gartner predicted that 50% of all companies in regulated industries would have a chief data officer (CDO) in 2017.[11] Even though this prediction may not have come true, the role of CDO has been on the rise for some years. The CDO should have the overarching responsibility for the organisation's data usage, data governance and data architecture. Their role may also include responsibility for data analytics as well as accountability for privacy and data protection on the C-suite level – something the DPO can never do as it would conflict with their obligation of integrity and their need to be free from conflict of interest.

Chief information security officer (CISO)

Introduced in the mid-1990s, the role of CISO is more widespread than that of DPO. As the DPO role becomes more common, the CISO and DPO will need to co-operate as they have slightly overlapping areas of responsibility. The CISO is, as the name reveals, the highest-ranking officer with responsibility for information security. In many organisations, the CISO will take care of the requirements relating to adequate security in Article 32 of the GDPR, but of course with an obligation to provide information to the DPO.

Legal counsel

The legal counsel supports an organisation's operational units and management with legal advice. It does not necessarily get involved operationally in the implementation of advice, but it may include individuals who support the business, taking a more hands-on approach by implementing advice and managing projects. In larger organisations, the legal function quite often has specialists in different legal fields, such as employment law, contract law and (for large multinational organisations) competition law.

Internal audit

As the role of the DPO has evolved from the EU Data Protection Directive to the GDPR, a larger amount of monitoring activity

---

11 Tom McCall (2015), 'Understanding the chief data officer role', *Gartner*, 18 February, www.gartner.com/smarterwithgartner/understanding-the-chief-data-officer-role.

has become required of the DPO. This does not mean the DPO must conduct all of these activities themselves; if your organisation has an internal audit function, its members will probably help with some of these tasks.[12]

Just like the DPO, the internal audit function should operate independently. However, in contrast to the DPO, the internal audit function can in most organisations be given instructions on areas to audit by the board of directors.

Customer service

Concerning an organisation's relationship with its consumers or users, the customer service department will be the first point of contact. It is advisable for service agents to take care of the most common data protection questions and only escalate more difficult questions to the DPO. In some organisations, service agents take care of questions but all complaints are forwarded to the DPO. Regardless of the split of responsibilities between the customer service department and the DPO, it should be a well-structured co-operation.

DPO RESPONSIBILITIES

We have previously in general terms discussed the mandatory tasks of the DPO as outlined in Article 39. These are:

- inform and advise;

- monitor compliance;

- provide advice regarding DPIAs;

- co-operate with data protection authorities;

- act as the contact point for EU data protection authorities;

- act as the contact point for data subjects.

---

12 See, for example, *Practice Advisory 2100-8: Internal auditing's role in evaluating an organization's privacy framework* (2005), Institute of Internal Auditors, https://www.tn.gov/content/dam/tn/tdot/documents/InternalAudit/IIA_Professional_Practices_Framework.pdf, p. 201.

In this section we will transform these tasks into actionable elements of your work. All your actions will require knowledge of your organisation and its business. This principle should act like a silver thread through all of your actions and assessments.

But first let's once more remind ourselves that the GDPR makes it very clear that it is always the controller, not the DPO, who is required to 'implement appropriate technical and organisational measures to ensure and to be able to demonstrate that processing is performed in accordance with this Regulation' (Article 24(1)).[13] Data protection compliance is the responsibility of the controller or processor, not the DPO.

Considering risks in everything you do

Knowledge of risk and risk assessments is fundamental to almost all requirements and obligations in the GDPR. Not even the rights of data subjects are absolute. Therefore, you need to consider risk in the execution of almost all of your tasks as a DPO. You must be able to consider the nature, scope, context and purposes of processing when performing your tasks (Article 39(2)). In the words of the WP29, DPOs should 'prioritise their activities and focus their efforts on issues that present higher data protection risks'.[14]

Some of the most important obligations under the GDPR relating to risk are:

- DPIAs (Article 35);

- data protection by design and by default (Article 25);

- data breach notifications (Article 33);

- security (Article 32).

---

13 Further, the DPO may not be subject to penalties for carrying out their tasks, as Article 38(3) requires that DPOs should 'not be dismissed or penalised by the controller or the processor for performing [their] tasks'.

14 Article 29 Working Party (2017), *Guidelines on Data Protection Officers ('DPOs')*, Directorate C of the European Commission, https://ec.europa.eu/newsroom/document.cfm?doc_id=44100, p. 18.

Chapter 3 considers the first three of these areas in more detail. Other areas that should also take account of risk are which internal training activities to provide to staff or management responsible for data processing activities, and which processing operations the DPO should devote more of their time and resources to.

The importance of understanding risk cannot be exaggerated. Therefore, Chapter 4 provides a thorough description of different types of risk and how to calculate risk.

Providing information and advice

As a DPO, you should make your organisation aware of its data protection obligations and responsibilities under the GDPR. First and foremost, this includes briefing management and informing other stakeholders of their data protection compliance obligations. This will be part of your proactive work, while monitoring and reporting will consist mostly of reactive elements.

Providing information and advice often means giving insight and guidance to the organisation so that its members can act and design products and services that measure up to the relevant legal and ethical standards. We believe being a DPO is about inspiring, guiding and supporting the organisation to have more and more integrity in its processes, services and strategy. Being proactive in this way is the best route to avoiding being pushed by a benevolent though somewhat clueless organisation to be completely reactive and prioritise based on your inbox. You are the expert on what constitutes product development (or the like) with integrity. A DPO is not there to hold endless Q&A sessions, nor to be an administrator of myriad Excel sheets!

Remember that you should give information and advice not only regarding the GDPR but also regarding all data protection obligations, including applicable national data protection law.

Monitoring compliance

Monitoring compliance and the effectiveness of your organisation's data protection practices is one of your main tasks, and it plays an important role in the organisation's ability to demonstrate accountability and provide evidence of compliance. A central part of this monitoring is to review your organisation and report non-compliance (and compliance!) to the highest management level in your organisation.

Just as information and advice must be given in the context of both international and national laws, the DPO should monitor compliance not only against the GDPR but also against applicable national data protection laws, as well as internal data protection policies. Article 39(1)(b) of the GDPR provides other examples of things the DPO should monitor, such as the assignment of responsibilities and training activities.

As mentioned, the compliance-monitoring requirement does not mean that the DPO is personally responsible when there is an instance of non-compliance. However, the DPO must inform management of non-compliance issues that they become aware of and probably also provide recommendations to mitigate any data protection gaps.

It should be emphasised that monitoring compliance with the GDPR should not be seen as a checklist or tick-box exercise. It is not possible to run through each of the requirements in the GDPR and simply tick a box stating 'done', and then deem the organisation to be fine and following the law. The aim is rather to push organisations to a cultural change and a more process-oriented way of working with data protection and privacy. Your monitoring and recommendations should facilitate your organisation's move towards such a cultural change.

On top of that, implementing data protection is not a one-off effort. It is a continual process that needs to be present at all times, throughout all parts of the organisation – not least for the business to be able to make the correct risk-based decisions. Consequently you, as the DPO, need to continually monitor the implementation of data protection and work with your organisation to interpret the requirements and obligations of the GDPR and other laws so that the organisation can find the best solution with minimal business disruption. This continual monitoring could well be done in a data protection programme, including annual controls and metrics.

Participating in data protection impact assessments

According to Article 35(1) of the GDPR, it is the task of the controller, not of the DPO, to carry out a DPIA (when necessary). However, the DPO can, and should, play a very important and useful role in assisting the controller. Article 35(2) specifically requires that the controller 'shall seek the advice' of the DPO when carrying out a DPIA and Article 39(1)(c) stipulates that one of the tasks of the DPO is to 'provide advice where requested as regards the data protection impact assessment and monitor its performance pursuant to Article 35'.

Concerning DPIAs, the WP29 recommends that:

The controller should seek the advice of the DPO, on the following issues, amongst others:

- whether or not to carry out a DPIA;

- what methodology to follow when carrying out a DPIA;

- whether to carry out the DPIA in-house or whether to outsource it;

- what safeguards (including technical and organisational measures) to apply to mitigate any risks to the rights and interests of the data subjects;

- whether or not the data protection impact assessment has been correctly carried out and whether its conclusions (whether or not to go ahead with the processing and what safeguards to apply) are in compliance with the GDPR.[15]

---

15 *Ibid*, p. 17.

If the controller disagrees with the advice provided by the DPO, the DPIA documentation should specifically justify in writing why the advice has not been actioned by the controller.

Valuable privacy control checklists to use when evaluating the security of data processing in the context of a DPIA can be found in:

- the ISO 27001 process;[16]
- the ISO 27002 privacy controls;[17]
- ISO/IEC 27701:2019 security techniques;[18]
- NIST SP 800-53 catalogues of privacy controls (free web resource).[19]

Acting as the contact point for data protection authorities

As the DPO, you will be the contact point for your organisation concerning all relevant data protection authorities. You should see this as co-operation and not a duty to give information to the authorities.

---

16 'ISO/IEC 27001: Information security management' (2020), International Organization for Standardization, https://www.iso.org/isoiec-27001-information-security.html.

17 'ISO/IEC 27002:2013: Information technology – Security techniques – Code of practice for information security controls' (2013), International Organization for Standardization, https://www.iso.org/standard/54533.html.

18 'ISO/IEC 27701:2019: Security techniques – Extension to ISO/IEC 27001 and ISO/IEC 27002 for privacy information management – Requirements and guidelines' (2019), International Organization for Standardization, https://www.iso.org/standard/71670.html.

19 'NIST special publication 800-53' (2020), National Institute of Standards and Technology, https://nvd.nist.gov/800-53.

In this capacity, you will provide a crucial link between your organisation and the data protection authorities. You will be responsible for describing the operations and business of the organisation, and you will therefore have the power to determine how your organisation is perceived by the authorities.

You will also be the point of contact if a case is raised in relation to your organisation. Some of the types of cases that might be raised are investigations, complaints and prior consultation (see Article 36 of the GDPR). The data protection authority will probably expect you as the DPO to have quite detailed knowledge of your organisation's business as well as its processing of personal data.

Sharing information with the authorities will be part of the co-operation. Depending on the case type, this could mean very little data or extensive descriptions of how your organisation operates. Some of this information will be critical business information or even trade secrets. Therefore, you must consult all relevant stakeholders before sharing any information.

It should also be noted that national legislation may preclude you from sharing certain types of information. Thus, the GDPR's co-operation requirement and sharing of information may be circumscribed by other applicable laws.

Acting in consultation with data protection authorities

According to Article 36 of the GDPR, the controller must consult the data protection authorities when a DPIA indicates a high risk to data subjects in the absence of mitigating actions. Article 39 states that the DPO should be the contact point for such consultations. It also stipulates an obligation for the DPO themselves to consult in other matters when appropriate. This obligation, according to the wording of the article, seems to be a stand-alone right of the DPO to consult the authorities without either notice or approval from the controller.

In many cases, a more suitable solution is informal consultations. Most authorities will try to help you out with your questions. If you do not want to disclose your identity, you can call the relevant authority's helpline without telling them your name or the organisation you work for, or you can engage an external counsel to ask for you. Most data protection authorities welcome informal contact and even encourage it as it creates better co-operation and a proactive environment. In many cases, these informal consultations can create trust between an organisation and the authorities. They can also prevent later enforcement actions.

Just as outlined above for other DPO responsibilities, the DPO might need to consider national legislation relating to legal privilege and other conflicting obligations concerning consultations with the authorities. Many countries have the principle of freedom of information, which makes it possible for the public to request any information provided to the authorities. You should therefore protect any confidential and sensitive information when communicating with the authorities. Seek legal advice if necessary.

Acting as the contact point for data subjects

A data subject may contact the DPO on all issues relating to the processing of their personal data. This includes, but is not restricted to, exercising their rights (e.g. the right to access or erasure of data). As stated above, it is probably good practice to let customer service be the first point of contact for consumers and users, instead of allowing them to reach the DPO directly. However, good business practice is to at least have a dedicated email address where data subjects can reach the DPO, even if it is the customer service department that receives and makes the first assessment of the message. Many, or even most, questions can probably be handled by customer service. You should together with customer service prepare template answers to the most common questions, and make sure every point of contact can recognise a data subject access request (DSAR) and know where to forward it. Another way of saving the DPO from being flooded with messages is to have a privacy portal where data subjects can themselves manage their privacy settings, ask for access and so on.

Organisations with external DPOs should clearly state in their service contract how external communications made on behalf of the organisation may be enacted by the DPO. It is important to note that being the contact point for data subjects is not the same thing as representing data subjects vis-à-vis the organisation.

Chapter 3 includes a more detailed discussion of data subjects' rights as stipulated in the GDPR.

Summary

In this section, we have taken a look at the mandatory tasks of the DPO and what they could mean in reality for you and your work. Some of the tasks could be delegated to other parts of the organisation and executed under your supervision (e.g. being the contact point for data subjects) whereas other tasks are probably best done by you (e.g. monitoring and reviewing compliance). In the next section, we will discuss how to govern the data protection practices in an organisation-wide data protection programme.

MANAGING THE DATA PROTECTION PROGRAMME

There are no legal regulations specifically on how to manage data protection compliance, and there is no GDPR standard you can straightforwardly implement. But common to all data protection programmes is that they should be tools or sets of processes that are used by the organisation to document, assess, monitor, enforce and improve the organisation's compliance with applicable data protection obligations. As such, they can also serve as tools for the DPO.

The data protection programme should balance applicable data protection requirements and expectations with the organisation's business strategy. A good programme is built on a sound understanding of business-critical data and of what the benefit of using such data is for the business and the data subjects; a further critical element is a willingness to continually improve practices and technology. Inspiration can be taken from recognised standards and frameworks, such as ISO 27701 and the Generally Accepted Privacy Principles (GAPP) (see Chapter 6). A good programme should integrate data protection requirements and representations into functional areas across the organisation.

Although dedicated projects will continue to be a useful method to allocate resources and achieve a large amount of work in a limited time frame, such initiatives should never drain resources or steal focus from long-term data protection management. The principle of accountability means that an organisation should have a formal process of data protection covering the whole organisation. The data protection programme is the framework for the long-term process.

The data protection programme should cover the data lifecycle, from governance of data protection to measuring, monitoring and reviewing programme performance. Figure 2.1 illustrates how developing your data protection programme will be an iterative process.

Figure 2.1 Developing a data protection programme

Improve

Implement

Develop

- Decide senior management ownership of privacy governance
- Decide on governance of data protection compliance
- Develop organisational privacy policies, processes and guidelines (internal framework)
- Define privacy programme activities, and actions

- Communicate the privacy programme to internal and external parties (internal privacy policy, external privacy notices and contracts)
- Ensure continual alignment of applicable laws, regulations and industry standards
- Roll out awareness education and training in new processes and GDPR requirements (individual rights, incidents)

- Continue to adapt the privacy programme to the company's developing business objectives
- New technology, new uses for data, potential mergers and acquisitions etc.
- Measure and evaluate the privacy programme's progress continually
- Do 'soft' and third-party audits of company's compliance

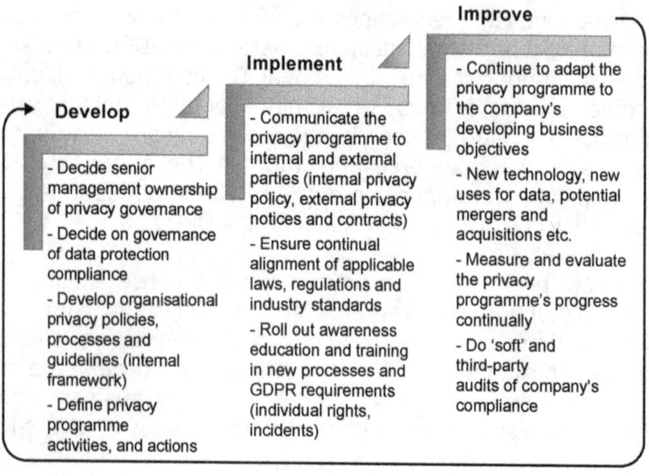

The elements of a data protection programme

As stated above, a data protection programme will consist of many different parts – for example, policies, procedures and training. As the programme develops, the parts will become more and more numerous, and it will be of the essence to bundle the parts into discrete elements. We suggest you categorise each aspect, part or action into one of the main elements from the very beginning.

The main elements of a data protection programme are:

1. **Data protection organisation**

   - How will top management be involved? Will the organisation be centralised or decentralised? Where does the DPO sit? (See the section 'Organisation' above.)

2. **Applicable laws, regulations and standards**

   - Taking stock of all applicable laws and requirements for your organisation is a gigantic task. By the time you are nearing completion, laws may have changed or your organisation may have amended its processes, making your compilation outdated. As a start to help you, especially with the jurisdiction foreign to yours, several global law firms maintain updated compilations of international data protection law trackers, available as web services. (See the section 'The European legal landscape' in Chapter 1. Also see Appendix 3.)

3. **Technical assessments of processing**

   - Technical assessments of data, such as DPIAs and privacy by design and by default. (See the sections 'Data protection impact assessment' and 'Data protection by design and by default' in Chapter 3.)

- Resources: the CNIL's PIA methodology[20] and the Privacy by Design framework of the European Union Agency for Cybersecurity (ENISA) (see Chapter 3).

4. Notices, policies and procedures

- External information and agreements such as a website privacy notice, a cookie policy and an external procedure to enable data subjects to request access to their personal data.

- Internal information and processes, such as an internal data protection policy, an IT policy, an IT security policy, an HR policy, and a retention, archival and destruction policy.

5. Training and awareness

- Awareness training, including raising awareness of data protection concepts and your organisation's data protection programme. (See the section 'Training and awareness' in Chapter 3.)

- Training staff in various practical processes and tasks relating to carrying out data protection obligations (e.g. identifying and managing a data protection complaint, or managing a potential personal data incident).

6. Protecting personal data

- Implementing appropriate technological security mechanisms for protecting personal data.

- Resources: the ISO 27001 standard (see Chapter 6) and ENISA's Privacy by Design framework (see Chapter 3).

7. Data breach incident plans

- Having a task force in place that can manage potential and actual personal data breaches.

---

20 'Privacy impact assessment' (2018), Commission Nationale de l'Informatique et des Libertés, https://www.cnil.fr/en/PIA-privacy-impact-assessment-en.

Setting up a data protection programme

The previous section described what elements should be part of a data protection programme. This section describes what to do when setting up a data protection programme. If you are taking over an existing data protection programme, you can use this guide to make sure nothing is missing by identifying gaps.

If you are newly appointed to the DPO role, it is good practice to begin with an audit (or a gap analysis) of your organisation's compliance – or, if you are established in the role, you could do this at the start (or end) of the calendar year. In some cases, it could very well be a gap analysis that convinces management that they should have a DPO in the first place.

Defining priorities and understanding business objectives

For your data protection programme to be effective, both you and the organisation should know what personal data is being processed, which legal obligations apply to this personal data, and how to most effectively and securely handle this data with the least amount of business disruption.

The level of the data protection programme is to a large extent determined by the organisation and top management's motivations for prioritising data protection in the organisation. These may include marketplace reputation and brand, ethical decision-making concerning the use of data, and safeguarding company confidential information against attacks and threats.

Regulated industries (such as financial and healthcare services) hold sensitive personal data, and the misuse of this data could affect their licence to operate. Additionally, industries without industry-specific data protection regulations, such as consumer-facing services and retailers, may hold vast amounts of personal data on their customers and are often subject to strict consumer and marketing legislation. Yet more industries process personal data, although this processing may not be as critical to their core business (e.g. in the case of manufacturing companies).

When setting up a data protection programme, make sure you understand your organisation's and top management's motives and drivers. As much as possible, you should also build your data protection programme on existing processes and ways of working.

Reviewing existing documentation and evidence

Before you begin to build your programme, you should do a gap analysis. This should consider both whether parts of the existing data protection programme have gaps and whether some core elements of a programme are missing entirely. For each item on the list, additional information should be included, such as responsible person, action items listed, status, deadline determined, cost estimated and dependencies.

A good starting point for a gap analysis is usually to read and understand relevant documentation. Special attention should be given to the internal data protection policy, the external data protection notice, the employee data protection notice, the ROPA and any descriptions of personal data flows.

All relevant documentation should be linked to the data protection programme. The programme should be the one-stop shop for all relevant documentation. However, this does not mean that the DPO owns the documents or their content.

Please note that this initial analysis is not a full review. Chapter 5 describes how to conduct such a review. At a later stage, you will need to assess and evaluate your organisation's actual practices against its written policies and agreed procedures.

Internal data protection policy   The internal data protection policy should stipulate how the organisation manages data protection and outline the structure of the data protection work. It should also guide all employees about the organisation's approach to data protection compliance.

The policy should include guiding principles that employees can understand and should on a general level describe the organisation's risk appetite. The policy should not be a guideline for the day-to-day data protection work in the organisation's various operational units or departments. For this, each unit or department should have a more detailed guideline that only relates to itself.

External (customer) and internal (employee) data protection notices

Transparency is a key concept in most data protection legislation and frameworks. The GDPR is no exception. The data protection notice should reflect all processing activities in a transparent and easy-to-understand way. You should do at least three assessments of the notice:

- Send the notice to all units and departments, and ask whether all of their processing is listed in the notice.
- Compare the ROPA with the notice. Do they correspond?
- Check whether all mandatory information is included in the notice.

For further information on the data protection notice, see the section 'Right to information' in Chapter 3.

Record of processing activities

The most important documentation is the record of processing activities (ROPA) (see Article 30 of the GDPR). This is further described in Chapter 3.

Your initial assessment of the register should first of all ensure that it includes all relevant fields. Next, you should make sure all common processing activities are included – for example, most organisations should have processing activities registered for sales, HR, product, marketing, business intelligence and analytics.

Preparing an action list

With your organisation's overall strategy in mind and on the basis of a current, in-depth knowledge of the trends in the industry, you can proceed to take stock of what to do. Keep in mind that it is not up to you to do everything on an action list; however, you should plan, anchor, monitor and follow up the necessary processes. That said, it is not your job to do the implementation – it is your job to monitor and ensure it is done. We would recommend implementing a responsibility assignment matrix to make the responsibilities clear internally.

Once you have done your initial assessments and have completed an analysis of possible compliance gaps, it is time to prioritise and create a list of suggested actions for your organisation. The order of the actions should be based on risk and targeting 'low-hanging fruit' (or quick wins). You will probably have found some gaps that could be closed relatively easily and within a short time frame. These actions could be marked as quick wins with short deadlines – for example, within one week, two weeks or a month. This will enable you to speedily show improvements and the necessity of the data protection programme.

It is important for the full list of suggested actions to be risk based, with the highest risk listed first. Identify which risks are actively enforced. Most often, data protection authorities have a publicly available enforcement agenda, and you should monitor this. At this stage, it might not be possible to set deadlines for all actions, but make sure you include a specified responsible person for each action.

You should also consider your organisation's ambition regarding data protection. Does it want to become an industry leader in data protection or merely do the least amount possible? This could affect both the actions themselves and the time frames for the actions. When you have created a draft action list, you need to engage with your internal stakeholders (including sales, product management, IT, HR, legal, procurement, business intelligence and business development) and ask them to provide input regarding their business priorities and deadlines for the actions.

The action list you initially create should be used to keep close track of the actions' implementation statuses and priorities. The key to solving data protection issues and building a successful data protection programme in the long term is to prioritise and plan effectively, and manage budgets and complex situations.

DPO's tips

Start small but build comprehensively when you create your data protection programme. Start with quick wins and focus on the highest priority and most high-risk activities. A quick win could be to review your online privacy notice and update it. Is it easy to locate and does it read well? Such things are easy to spot for the professional and a good place to start in improving business compliance and developing trust with consumers. Going after the low-hanging fruit will also help you to collect early wins and produce results that you can report upwards.

Moving from the initial phase to business as usual

At some point, you will need to move on from the execution of the initial action list and begin to run your organisation's data protection on a more ongoing basis. Even though this process is also about actions, it has more of a recurring nature than actions targeted at closing compliance gaps. Doing a gap analysis and creating action lists should not constitute the main body of your data protection programme.

When your data protection programme has become business as usual, it will consist of many ongoing controls and activities. At this stage, the programme has no start or end date, but it is still important to show progress and collect evidence that the programme is evolving. Therefore, it will be important to establish and demonstrate the maturity of the data protection programme, and how it is developing over time.

Assessing the maturity level

Why do we talk about data protection maturity? Well, assessing and measuring the implementation of good data protection practices is the best way to evidence that an organisation is operating with managed risk. Compliance is not the same thing as having documentation in place or keeping it updated; it is about having the correct requirements and instructions in your documentation and making sure everyone abides by them.

Evaluating the maturity of a data protection programme is not about assessing the effectiveness of the programme; it is about assessing how developed its governance structure is. That being said, it is also valuable to assess the effectiveness of the programme, as this will tell you how good the elements of the programme are at preventing data protection incidents from occurring and mitigating them if they do occur. See the next section for more on metrics that can be used for this purpose.

The difference between the maturity level and effectiveness of a programme can most easily be described by using the example of data protection training. An indication of a higher maturity level might be that all new employees participate in data protection training within one month of joining the organisation as part of the onboarding process. However, establishing that there is a process in place and that it is followed does not say anything definitive about the effectiveness of the training.

To evaluate a data protection programme's maturity, you could use established programme maturity levels. These are criteria that are commonly used to evaluate where a programme sits in terms of maturity. Understanding your data protection programme's maturity level will help the organisation and you to prioritise the development of the programme and could be an efficient way to benchmark your organisation in relation to other organisations in your industry.

Most maturity models consist of five levels: initial/ad hoc, repeatable, defined, managed and optimised (see Table 2.1). Using these maturity levels and the GAPP principles (see Chapter 6), you can create a matrix to assess each area of your privacy programme.

Table 2.1 Maturity levels of a data protection programme

Maturity level	General description
Initial/ad hoc	Actions are mainly done on an ad hoc basis. A lot of work consists of putting out fires as they occur. There are no processes and almost nothing is documented. Such programmes are often highly dependent on certain key individuals knowing how to act.
Repeatable	The basic elements, processes and procedures are in place, as are the most essential steering documents (e.g. the internal data protection policy). However, the policies do not cover all necessary elements, are incomplete and/or are partly incorrect.
Defined	The programme uses best practices and standards. Controls are implemented and the organisation follows guidelines.
Managed	Metrics are used to increase the performance of the programme over time. Reporting is done in a structured and well-defined way. Decisions are executed according to defined processes. Processes are monitored and the overall data protection programme is in place and is working.
Optimised	The programme is a self-playing piano that is continually evolving, and compliance is a competitive advantage.

Using metrics to improve performance

Metrics are quantifiable parameters or measures used to assess, compare, or track performance or production. As you will know by now, the GDPR not only imposes many requirements and obligations on actual data processing but also imposes an obligation on all organisations to be able to demonstrate compliance. This is where metrics can play a crucial role. They can help you to track your organisation's compliance over time.

Because they can be transformed into diagrams and coloured charts in presentations, metrics can also be an excellent way of demonstrating the effectiveness of a data protection programme to stakeholders and top management. This is important regarding the budget for the programme. These stakeholders will not care much about the actual legal requirements and thus it will be much more useful to have a few slides with diagrams and graphs based on metrics.

Choosing metrics
What you should measure depends on your organisation and its maturity level. Finding metrics that are relevant and beneficial for an organisation can be difficult; thus, you should refine them over time and not be afraid to change them when necessary. A commonly used acronym for how to choose metrics is SMART. It stands for specific, measurable, achievable, relevant and time-bound.[21] All your metrics should meet these qualifications. (There is more about SMART in Appendix 2.)

Furthermore, all metrics should be relevant to your organisation and preferably answer questions you anticipate your stakeholders will ask. Do not choose metrics just because you can measure something; instead, pick the most relevant

---

[21] There are slight variations in what the letters stand for. Most notably, the letter A can also refer to 'accurate' and the letter R to 'realistic'. SMART is normally attributed to Peter Drucker (1954), *The Practice of Management*, New York: Harper.

metrics and make them of high quality. With this in mind, keep it simple. Don't let your relevant metrics be overshadowed by the use of several irrelevant metrics just because these were easy to collect.

Some areas where metrics could be useful are training of employees, DSARs, and data protection incidents and breaches.

Training People are the number one key to success. Thus, data protection awareness among employees is very important. Without this awareness, other initiatives will probably fail. This is why it is so important to keep track of training that is conducted. The most basic metrics are the number of training courses conducted and the percentage of employees who have completed the training. A slightly more advanced metric could be how much time passes between onboarding employees and completing their training. You could also slice this information up to compare different business units and departments.

Data subject access requests We believe that the number of DSARs will increase over time for most organisations. Whether this is true or not can only be proved using metrics. There are various aspects of DSARs that can be measured as metrics. Some examples could be the number of requests, the time to reply or the number of complaints received following DSARs. Such metrics can be used in budget discussions regarding the automation of this process. At some point, it may be worth investing in fully or semi-automated processes for DSARs, depending on the size of your company. These can collect the requested data and, in some cases, also be used for the administration of the requests.

Types and number of data protection incidents, including data protection breaches In the domain of information security, it has for a long time been best practice to categorise incidents by type, not least because this helps in prioritising actions. It is time for data protection to copy this practice and start to categorise data protection incidents by type. This will also help you concerning the GDPR requirement regarding notification of personal data breaches.

DPO's tips

- Help management to define their privacy vision. The objective of any compliance programme is to help the organisation to become better, not to realise your 'perfect' vision (keep in mind expertise bias – i.e. be aware that you may have a personal preference towards a favoured outcome and this may influence you disproportionately).

- Build something manageable. Build the data protection programme in phases together with the business, so that it is business priorities that are driving the change.

- Easy is good and early wins are motivating. Review and update your online information documents. Look at what your main competitors are doing and adapt this to your practices, applying sound judgement.

- Done is better than perfect. Keep track of your task list on the one hand and big-picture issues on the other.

- Find the right approach for your organisation – balance being proactive with being reactive. Ensure you have a budget for developing your own competence from HR (if you are an internal DPO) or in your service contract (if you are an external DPO).

SUMMARY

In this chapter, we have discussed how to kick-start your assignment as a DPO and how to set up a sustainable data protection programme. The data protection programme should balance applicable data protection requirements and expectations with the organisation's business strategy. Do a thorough review of any existing programmes and practices. As a DPO, you will see success if you can take a long-term view, building effective processes that engage the rest of the organisation while addressing ad hoc gaps and events according to an action plan.

We have also thoroughly outlined what the typical tasks of a DPO are and what they are not. And we have provided some suggestions for metrics you and your organisation can use to take the temperature of your data protection practices over time.

3 THE DATA PROTECTION PROCESSES

The General Data Protection Regulation (GDPR) imposes several obligations on controllers (some of these also apply to processors). We believe these obligations should be handled by either incorporating them into existing processes or adding new specific processes. The latter course of action should only be applied when no suitable processes exist. It will not be a sustainable solution to act on these obligations in an ad hoc manner or try to set them up in a rush, in case there is an audit or a data subject exerts one of their rights. Setting up these processes is an obligation of the organisation, but the data protection officer (DPO) needs to understand and be able to advise on them. Therefore, we will briefly examine them in this chapter.

Sustainable business practice needs three components to work in a compliant manner: people, processes and systems. If one or more is missing, it is likely the compliance work will fail. For example, an organisation must make sure the systems support the actual processes; otherwise, employees will find their own solutions. And if the organisation doesn't train its employees, they will make up their own ad hoc processes.

TRAINING AND AWARENESS

Out of the three components listed above, people are by far the most important. They are also the single most important factor in working proactively, by creating a culture of data protection and making data protection something that is considered in the day-to-day operations of the organisation and intertwined in its spinal cord.

It is the organisation that is responsible for having proper processes for training staff and also making sure the training is thorough enough. However, in many organisations, training is executed by the DPO. Additionally, it is the DPO's responsibility to assess and monitor the compliance of the training (see Article 39(1) of the GDPR).

All employees[1] and consultants should receive general data protection training as early as possible, potentially even during onboarding. Also, they should receive targeted training relevant to their specific working tasks. The initial training should be supported by recurring training and awareness-raising activities.

In our experience, classroom training is most efficient, but it can be hard to conduct in large or geographically widespread organisations. In those cases, off-the-shelf e-training could be a better solution. Most of these training courses can be customised in terms of both content and branding to fit the organisation.

The DPO should make sure the cost of training is not allocated to their budget. On the other hand, some of the awareness-raising activities may be both decided and executed by the DPO and should thus be in the DPO's budget.

RECORD OF PROCESSING ACTIVITIES

The core data protection documentation for any organisation should be its record of processing activities (ROPA). Every instance of processing of personal data should be registered in the ROPA. The ROPA is a data and processing inventory, and if thoroughly done it should serve as the single point of knowledge if you or anyone else wants to get an exhaustive view of what personal data your organisation is processing and for what purposes. The legal requirements for the ROPA are described in Article 30 of the GDPR.

---

1   This includes everyone from management downwards.

Some organisations might need two ROPAs, one for processing operations where the organisation is the controller (Article 30(1)) and another for processing operations carried out on behalf of the organisation's client as a processor (Article 30(2)). Following are the requirements for controllers in Article 30(1) of the GDPR as an example:

- description of processing;
- identity of the data controller, and whether they are jointly responsible;
- name and contact details of the DPO;
- purposes of processing – main purpose and sub-purposes;
- security measures – technical and organisational measures;
- categories of data concerned, such as common personal data (e.g. civil status, personal life), data perceived as sensitive (e.g. economic and financial information), online identifiers or location data;
- time limit for the deletion of data per category of data;
- details of sensitive data (formally 'special category' data; see Chapter 1), including such things as individuals' unique national identification number and political opinion;
- categories of data subjects;
- recipients of the data;
- transfers outside the EU or European Economic Area (EEA) – recipient, country and type of transfer mechanism.

To achieve good governance of an organisation's personal data, additional non-mandatory information should be added to the ROPA. For example, the ROPA should have cross-references between related entries and the organisation's contract database, if applicable. Furthermore, all records should have a designated responsible department or unit. The ROPA should also, if possible, have references to the IT systems in which the processing takes place for each entry.

Administrating the ROPA and keeping it up to date across the organisation is often quite a complicated and time-consuming task. It should be stressed that this should not be the responsibility of the DPO. In our opinion, keeping the ROPA complete and up to date is a responsibility that lies entirely with the organisation, even though the DPO may have valuable suggestions for improvement. According to the European Data Protection Board (EDPB), 'nothing prevents the controller or the processor from assigning the DPO with the task of maintaining the record of processing operations under the responsibility of the controller or the processor'.[2] However, in our view, maintaining the ROPA only relates to the framework and system, not the content, since the latter would be a conflict of interest. Instead, a good solution for most organisations is to internally delegate the responsibility for updating the ROPA to the head of the assigned department or unit. To ensure a high-quality ROPA, we suggest including the DPO in the process for new registrations and updates to the registry. In large organisations, it may be necessary to delegate this task to another person with deep data protection knowledge.

It will be difficult to strike the balance between having as much information as possible but not more than the organisation can manage to keep up to date. Therefore, the registry should be designed with great care right from the start. Several regulators have published guidelines on ROPAs that can be used as a reference – for example:

- **Belgian data protection authority:** 'Model voor een Register van de verwerkingsactiviteiten' (Model for a Register of Processing Operations);[3]

---

2 Article 29 Working Party (2017), *Guidelines on Data Protection Officers ('DPOs')*, Directorate C of the European Commission, https://ec.europa.eu/newsroom/document.cfm?doc_id=44100, p. 19.

3 See https://www.ccvs.be/index.php/de/ma-information/menu-legislation/207-model-voor-een-register-van-de-verwerkingsactiviteiten.

- **French data protection authority:** *General Data Protection Regulation Guide for Processors* and sample record;[4]

- **German Conference of Independent Federal and State Data Protection Authorities (Datenschutzkonferenz):** sample records controller and sample records processor.[5]

Take it as a rule of thumb to make sure your organisation does not register IT systems or databases in the ROPA. Register processing activities and all of the purposes.

DATA PROTECTION IMPACT ASSESSMENTS

Performing and advising on various risk assessments relating to data protection will likely be one of your most common tasks as a DPO. This section provides an overview of data protection impact assessments (DPIAs), looks into their background, discusses when they are needed and what they contain, and examines how to set them up.

Overview of DPIAs

A DPIA, also known as a privacy impact assessment (PIA), is a formal process for identifying data protection risks and mitigating actions in a business context. Due to the GDPR's principle of accountability (see Chapter 1), the process needs to be properly documented.

The risk assessment starts with scoping: what are the fundamentals of the processing at hand? The next stage is to

---

4   See https://www.cnil.fr/sites/default/files/atoms/files/rgpd-guide_sous-traitant-cnil_en.pdf and https://www.cnil.fr/sites/default/files/atoms/files/registre-reglement-publie.xlsx.

5   See www.alstonprivacy.com/wp-content/uploads/2018/02/DSK-Sample-Processing-Record_Controller_EN_HL.docx and www.alstonprivacy.com/wp-content/uploads/2018/02/DSK-Sample-Processing-Record_Processor_EN_HL.docx.

assess risks and technical safeguards, and this is followed by the assessment itself and advice from the DPO on the overall level of compliance. We strongly recommend including a step that makes the organisation take responsibility for the process before submitting its findings to the highest level of management for validation.

Background

The DPIA process (see Figure 3.1) was not introduced by the GDPR; rather, it has existed for quite a long time. There are some excellent guidelines in existence, for example from Canada[6] and the UK.[7] However, the DPIA process as introduced by the GDPR is new to the extent that the DPO must advise on the process and the controller or processor must validate the findings. The validation part of the DPIA process should be seen as a manifestation of the new principle of accountability.

Figure 3.1 An overview of the DPIA process

Process owner	Chief information security officer	Data protection officer	Process owner	Highest management
Fundamentals	**IT risks**	**Data protection risks**	**Implementation plan**	**Validation**
Justification	Technical controls	Data flow	Action plan	Decision
Context	Organisational controls	Harms	Investment required	Conditions
Data flow	controls	Consultation	Alternatives	Risk acceptance
Harms		Advice	Costs	
		Input to validation	Risks	

---

6 'Expectations: OPC's guide to the privacy impact assessment process' (2020), Office of the Privacy Commissioner of Canada, https://www.priv.gc.ca/en/privacy-topics/privacy-impact-assessments/gd_exp_202003.

7 *Conducting Privacy Impact Assessments Code of Practice* (2020), Information Commissioner's Office, https://ico.org.uk/media/about-the-ico/consultations/2052/draft-conducting-privacy-impact-assessments-code-of-practice.pdf.

When is a DPIA needed?

According to Article 35 of the GDPR, a DPIA is mandatory if data processing is 'likely to result in a high risk to the rights and freedoms of natural persons'. The Article 29 Working Party (WP29) has released a guideline to clarify which processing operations require a DPIA. According to the WP29, factors considered to elevate risk to individuals are:

- large-scale processing;
- processing targeting vulnerable persons;
- use of untested technology or organisational solutions;
- processing of sensitive data;
- combination/matching of separate databases;
- automated decision-making significantly affecting individuals;
- evaluations of data subjects;
- cross-border transfers;
- processing that prevents data subjects from exercising a right or using a service or a contract.[8]

All national data protection authorities have published guidelines for when a DPIA should be conducted. Your organisation should consult all relevant national guidelines as they differ slightly in scope. The European Data Protection Supervisor had also published material about DPIAs.[9]

---

[8] Article 29 Working Party (2017), *Guidelines on Data Protection Impact Assessment (DPIA) and Determining whether Processing is 'Likely to Result in a High Risk' for the Purposes of Regulation 2016/679*, Directorate C of the European Commission, https://ec.europa.eu/newsroom/article29/item-detail.cfm?item_id=611236, p. 9.

[9] For example, see *Accountability on the Ground Part II: Data Protection Impact Assessments & Prior Consultation* (2018), European Data Protection Supervisor, https://edps.europa.eu/sites/edp/files/publication/18-02-06_accountability_on_the_ground_part_2_en.pdf.

What should be in a DPIA?

On the general level, a DPIA should consist of at least the following elements:

- context and description of the processing;
- a description of the legal basis – for example, a legitimate interests assessment (LIA) if applicable;
- how each of the fundamental data protection principles is met;
- an assessment of the data protection risks, including mitigating measures;
- security of processing;
- DPO advice (if applicable);
- consultation with the lead supervisory authority (if applicable);
- validation by the representative of the controller or processor (most often the process, product or system owner).

Great work has been done by the supervisory authorities on providing guidance and examples of good-enough DPIA models. The French data protection authority, the Commission Nationale de l'Informatique et des Libertés (CNIL), has published an ambitious set of handbooks on DPIAs containing a methodology, knowledge bases on security guidance, templates and an example of a connected object.[10] The UK Information Commissioner's Office (ICO) has published good materials as well, particularly if you are interested in a more 'light' version of risk assessment.[11]

---

10 'Privacy impact assessment' (2018), Commission Nationale de l'Informatique et des Libertés, https://www.cnil.fr/en/PIA-privacy-impact-assessment-en.

11 'Sample DPIA template (v 0.4 20180622)' (2018), Information Commissioner's Office, https://ico.org.uk/media/for-organisations/documents/2553993/dpia-template.docx. See also the guidance 'How do we do a DPIA?' (n.d.), Information Commissioner's Office, https://ico.org.uk/for-organisations/guide-to-data-protection/guide-to-the-general-data-protection-regulation-gdpr/data-protection-impact-assessments-dpias/how-do-we-do-a-dpia.

Remember to use the body of work of relevant ISO standards (see Chapter 6) and the various guides to information security and privacy by default and by design from the European Union Agency for Cybersecurity (ENISA) (see the section 'ENISA's Privacy by Design framework' later in this chapter) when you assess the technical aspects of the processing at hand.

Also central to being able to consider the potential threats and harms to affected data subjects are the concepts of privacy threats, 'unjustifiable collection',[12] 'inappropriate use'[13] and 'security breaches'. Privacy harms include tangible harms (such as bodily harm, loss of liberty and financial loss) and intangible harms (such as excessive surveillance, suppression of free speech or free association, anxiety, discrimination, excessive state power and loss of social trust). For more information on privacy threats and harms, see the report *Risk, High Risk, Risk Assessments and Data Protection Impact Assessments under the GDPR* by the Centre for Information Policy and Leadership.[14]

Setting up a DPIA

It is a big mistake for a DPO to initiate and launch a DPIA. The risk assessment should be a complex discussion between internal process owners, where their concerns are balanced against the level of risk that the organisation can accept. These concerns will vary over time and according to the processing at hand and its value to the organisation. This discussion is too important for the DPO to monopolise. If the DPO 'owns' the process, there is a high risk that the process (and the DPO) will be marginalised in the organisation.

---

12 This means the collection of personal data that is unlawful – for example, the wrong legal basis is used or too much data is collected.

13 This means the use is against the fundamental data protection principles in Article 5 of the GDPR.

14 *Risk, High Risk, Risk Assessments and Data Protection Impact Assessments under the GDPR* (2016), Centre for Information Policy Leadership, https://www. huntonprivacyblog.com/wp-content/uploads/sites/28/2016/12/cipl_gdpr_project_ risk_white_paper_21_december_2016.pdf.

DPO's tips

In our experience, it is advisable to adapt the formal legal DPIA process (see the previous sections) to the reality in which we live and work. Hence, add a step in the DPIA process that lets the initiator of the DPIA (process owner or system owner) have a say and suggest an action plan after the DPO provides their advice but **before** the DPIA is sent for approval or dismissal by the deciding body. Adding the possibility for a process or system owner to learn, adapt and expand on the overall advice and assessment makes a DPIA truly effective and will take you further in fulfilling your objective – to improve your organisation's data protection compliance (albeit one step at a time).

Identifying, assessing and mitigating data protection risk is one of the most powerful processes you as a DPO will be entrusted with. It is powerful because it can bring the organisation together around its data protection strategy and give the organisation the tools to drive change. If implemented poorly, though, it will create lots of administrative work for the DPO and frustration for the management.

The most efficient (and data protection mature) organisations have implemented risk assessment actions across the organisation as part of their data governance process. In essence, the organisation itself has checklists and processes that identify the need for a risk assessment (whether a new one or an update of an existing assessment). The various process owners and system owners lead the work of getting the risk assessment done and involve the DPO and other domain experts (HR, internal legal, IT security, etc.) where necessary. The outcome of the risk assessment has the support of the affected process owners and system owners, who will have to implement any corrective measures in order to proceed. Formal approval will be provided by a committee or person entrusted by the board of directors. A decision is much easier to obtain if it is clear that the organisation is behind it.

DPO's tips

Since DPIAs deal with data protection risks (i.e. risks to data subjects) and not other commercial or corporate risks, we have found that it can be hard to explain DPIAs to executives and to link them to existing risk management systems in organisations. One way of getting the attention and understanding of executives is to link data protection risks to corporate risks – for example, how the organisation's brand and reputation could be affected if it exposes individuals to high data protection risks.

Most often, however, it is clear to the executives on a compliance committee that if a risk assessment classifies a new global HR system (for example) as a security risk if several mitigating actions are not taken, it is a no-go. An HR director is unlikely to implement such a solution in good conscience and risk undermining their influence with the employees. (Not to mention that the employees may initiate legal action against the employer.)

DATA PROTECTION BY DESIGN AND BY DEFAULT

In the mid-1990s, Dr Ann Cavoukian, at the time Information and Privacy Commissioner of Ontario, introduced the concept of privacy by design.[15] She intended to develop privacy and data protection from a tick-box compliance exercise to the default way of operation in an organisation. The idea of data protection by design and by default is based on seven foundational principles that should pervade the whole organisation and the entire information lifecycle. These are:

- Proactive not Reactive; Preventative not Remedial;
- Privacy as the Default Setting;

---

15 A. Cavoukian (2010), 'Privacy by design: the definitive workshop. A foreword by Ann Cavoukian, Ph.D', *Identity in the Information Society* 3, 247–251.

- Privacy Embedded into Design;
- Full Functionality – Positive-Sum, not Zero-Sum;
- End-to-End Security – Full Lifecycle Protection;
- Visibility and Transparency – Keep it Open;
- Respect for User Privacy – Keep it User-Centric.[16]

The main aim is to prevent harm by changing the focus from reactivity to proactivity. The concept also includes the practice of embedding privacy measures and privacy-enhancing technologies (PETs) directly into the design of information technologies and systems.

Ever since the concept's introduction, data protection authorities in the EU have preached in favour of its use. But it wasn't codified in the Data Protection Directive. Rather, it was mentioned as one way of fulfilling the other stipulated requirements and obligations. However, the obligation to adopt data protection by design and by default has now been codified in Article 25 of the GDPR. When an organisation implements data protection by design and by default, it should consider the current technologies available, the cost of implementation, and the nature, scope, context and purposes of the processing, and balance these against the risks, considering the likelihood and potential severity of harm to data subjects. The mitigation actions taken may include technical and/or organisational measures.

Examples of data protection by design

- Privileged access
- Screen protection

---

16 A. Cavoukian (2011), *Privacy by Design: The 7 Foundational Principles*, Information and Privacy Commissioner of Ontario, https://www.ipc.on.ca/wp-content/uploads/resources/7foundationalprinciples.pdf.

- 'Just-in-time' notice that is revealed when triggered by a user's actions

- Privacy notice one click away

Examples of data protection by default

- Unticked boxes as the default

- Privacy-friendly default settings – for example, by having radio buttons in 'off' mode

- The strictest possible access restrictions as the default

ENISA's Privacy by Design framework

In 2014, ENISA published a comprehensive guide to the concept in its *Privacy and Data Protection by Design: From Policy to Engineering*.[17] This report is recommended for its detailed inventory of existing approaches, strategies and technical mechanisms relating to privacy by design.

ENISA mentions eight privacy design strategies[18] that can be used to adhere to the principle of data protection by design and by default in Article 25 of the GDPR (see the following box).

---

17 G. Danezis et al. (2014), *Privacy and Data Protection by Design: From Policy to Engineering*, European Union Agency for Cybersecurity, https://www.enisa.europa.eu/publications/privacy-and-data-protection-by-design.

18 See 'Privacy by design' (2020), ENISA, https://www.enisa.europa.eu/topics/data-protection/privacy-by-design.

ENISA's privacy design strategies[19]

- **Minimise:** the amount of personal data that is processed shall be restricted to the minimal amount possible. Examples of common design patterns are 'select before you collect', anonymisation and the use of pseudonyms.

- **Hide**: personal data and its interrelationships should be hidden from plain view to lessen the risk of abuse and misuse. Examples include using encryption of data, mixing networks to hide traffic patterns and unlinking related events (such as attribute-based credentials[20]).

- **Separate**: personal data should be processed in a distributed manner, in separate compartments where possible, instead of using more centralised solutions.

- **Aggregate:** personal data should be processed at the highest possible level of aggregation with the least possible detail to enable it to be useful. Examples include aggregation over time, dynamic location granularity, differential privacy and other anonymisation techniques.

- **Inform:** data subjects should be adequately informed if their personal data is processed. Examples include data breach notifications and providing a platform where data subjects can make choices about their privacy preferences.

- **Control:** data subjects should be provided with agency over the processing of their personal

---

19 Adapted with permission from ENISA (*ibid.*, pp. 18–22).

20 See S. Krenn et al. (2017), 'Towards attribute-based credentials in the cloud' in *CANS 2017: Cryptology and Network Security*, edited by S. Capkun and S. S. M. Chow (pp. 179–202), Cham: Springer.

data. Examples include using user-centric identity management and end-to-end encryption support control.

- **Enforce:** a legally valid data protection policy should be in place and enforced. Examples include policies and just-in-time pop-ups with a privacy notice or cookie policy information.

- **Demonstrate:** the data controller is obligated to demonstrate compliance with the internal data protection policy and applicable legal requirements. This principle supports the GDPR's notion of accountability. To apply this principle, you must have a suitable governance structure and documented evidence of how your internal data protection policy is effectively implemented in your organisation and the relevant IT systems. Examples include privacy management systems and the use of logging techniques and processes and auditing.

Privacy-enhancing technologies

A subgenre of data protection by design on the technology side is privacy-enhancing technologies (PETs). The concept of PETs was created around 20 years ago, but there is still no uniform definition. Typically, the term refers to a broad range of technologies that are designed to support privacy and data protection. At first, PETs were focused on various techniques for data minimisation and/or encryption. Even though this is still part of the concept, other areas have been added.

Today, PETs focus more on empowering individuals with various control mechanisms. An example is user portals that enable data subjects to review their personal data and/or settings, enabling them to control for what purposes their personal data is processed.

Examples of privacy-enhancing technologies

- Encryption
- Anonymisation
- Obfuscation
- Network protection – VCNs (virtual cloud networks), firewalls and so on
- Identity and access management
- Data subject privacy settings
- Data minimisation

We recommend that you prioritise understanding the basic technicalities of the fundamental PETs listed in the box above. Central to your reading list should be the WP29's opinion on anonymisation techniques.[21] However, time is a critical factor and you would be wise to stay updated on the latest technological advancements, as these may render some techniques out of date and ineffective. According to a scientific study by researchers at Imperial College London, current methods of anonymising personal data may leave individuals at risk of being re-identified. Merely sampling or aggregating data is not enough. The study found that 99.8% of Americans could be correctly re-identified in an anonymised data set by using 15 characteristics such as age, gender and marital status.[22]

---

21 Article 29 Working Party (2014), *Opinion 05/2014 on Anonymisation Techniques*, Directorate C of the European Commission, https://ec.europa.eu/justice/article-29/documentation/opinion-recommendation/files/2014/wp216_en.pdf.

22 L. Rocher, J. M. Hendrickx and Y.-A. de Montjoye (2019), 'Estimating the success of re-identifications in incomplete datasets using generative models', *Nature Communications* 10, 3069.

THE USE OF PROCESSORS

Most organisations cannot host and run all necessary services or applications by themselves. Instead, they need to use service providers specialising in certain fields, such as HR applications or mail applications. Another reason to use service providers is scalability. In most cases, it is both easier and faster to upgrade to a higher service level via a provider than to upgrade internal systems or services.

In terms of processors, providers can be divided into the following groups:

- Software as a Service (SaaS) – for example, PayPal and Zendesk;

- Infrastructure as a Service (IaaS) – for example, Amazon Web Services;

- Platform as a Service (PaaS) – for example, Salesforce.

If a controller uses any of these for processing personal data, the vendor will by definition be a processor. According to Article 28 of the GDPR:

> The controller shall use only processors providing sufficient guarantees to implement appropriate technical and organisational measures in such a manner that processing will meet the requirements of this Regulation and ensure the protection of the rights of the data subject.

This entails that the controller must assess the vendor before engaging it. Before processing by processors starts, the controller must also enter into a contract with the processor – specifically, a data processing agreement.[23] The data processing agreement should cover all relevant aspects of what and how the processor will process the personal data on behalf of the controller.

---

23 The data processing agreement is often referred to as a 'DPA' by lawyers. Be aware that data protection authorities are also sometimes referred to as 'DPAs'.

If a controller uses processors outside the EU, additional requirements apply. For the data transfer to the processor to be legal, one of the exceptions to the general prohibition on the transfer of personal data outside the EU must apply. For processors, this is normally solved through one of the following:

- the data processing agreement including EU Standard Contractual Clauses (covered later in this chapter);
- the vendor processing personal data in a country with adequate data protection according to a decision by the European Commission.

Further information on the international transfer of personal data is provided later in this chapter.

Onboarding of processors

As stated above, a controller may only use a processor that provides 'sufficient guarantees to implement appropriate technical and organisational measures in such a manner that processing will meet the requirements of this Regulation and ensure the protection of the rights of the data subject' (Article 28 of the GDPR). This is the case for all processors, current and future. There are no excuses for not performing a basic assessment of existing processors.

It is your job as the DPO to ensure that only vendors that meet these standards are used and that proper data processing agreements are in place. To ease your burden, a good practice is to help your organisation's procurers to set up checklists and templates. Furthermore, you can help by setting up questionnaires to be sent to processors. You should also list a few red flags your staff should look for.

Continual review

Even when your organisation has done thorough due diligence during boarding, it is still necessary to continually evaluate your processors. A good practice is to decide the frequency during onboarding – for example, annual or bi-annual reviews.

You could also decide to do various kinds of review. Three examples of review types are:

- on-site;
- new questionnaire;
- data processing agreement review.

From time to time it will also be necessary to do ad hoc reviews – for example, if it becomes known that the processor has had a security breach or personal data incident.

Bear in mind too that all decisions regarding the type of review and frequency should be risk based, and all data processing agreements must include audit rights.

Offboarding of processors

Eventually, your organisation will terminate its contract with a processor. It is important the data processing agreement contains specifications for this case and regulates what should happen at the termination of the contract. Normally the controller should be entitled to either have all its data exported in a standard readable format or have all its data deleted – whatever the controller chooses.

A common challenge during offboarding is the lock-in effect – that is, the difficulties of changing from one service provider to another. If your organisation intends to transfer current personal data from the first provider to the new provider, it is important to take measures to ascertain that no personal data is destroyed, altered or corrupted.

SHARING AND INTERNATIONAL TRANSFER OF PERSONAL DATA

First of all, it is important to separate sharing of data from international transfer of data. Sharing of personal data is always done to an external party, while international transfers may be done within the organisation or externally.

Sharing of personal data

Sharing of data is considered to be processing of data, and as such must have a legal basis. In most cases the sharing is a secondary purpose, and as such it may not rely on the same legal basis as the main purpose.

International transfer of personal data

The GDPR is not just about protecting data subjects' personal data; it is also about the free movement of that same personal data. Recital 3 of the GDPR states that the regulation is intended to ensure the free flow of personal data between the member states. In contrast, the transfer of personal data outside the EU is regulated by a whole chapter of the GDPR (Chapter 5). The basic principle is that transfers are prohibited. However, there are exceptions to the prohibition. Most of the exceptions are similar to the transfer rules in the Data Protection Directive. The main conditions under which transfer is allowed are if there is an 'adequacy decision' by the European Commission or if appropriate safeguards are provided.

Adequacy decision by the European Commission
Transfer of personal data to a third country may take place if the European Commission has decided that the third country (or one or more specified sectors within the third country in question) ensures an adequate level of protection. Examples of such countries are Argentina, Israel, Japan and New Zealand.

Appropriate safeguards are provided
Transfer of personal data to a third country may take place if the appropriate safeguards are provided. According to Article 46 of the GDPR:

The appropriate safeguards... may be provided... by:

(a) a legally binding and enforceable instrument between public authorities or bodies;

(b) binding corporate rules...;

(c) standard data protection clauses adopted by the Commission...;

(d) standard data protection clauses adopted by a supervisory authority and approved by the Commission...;

(e) an approved code of conduct... together with binding and enforceable commitments of the controller or processor in the third country to apply the appropriate safeguards, including as regards data subjects' rights; or

(f) an approved certification mechanism... together with binding and enforceable commitments of the controller or processor in the third country to apply the appropriate safeguards, including as regards data subjects' rights.

On top of that, some conditions apply for 'singular' transfers. Article 49 of the GDPR indicates that these should be used carefully:

In the absence of an adequacy decision... or of appropriate safeguards... a transfer or a set of transfers of personal data to a third country or an international organisation shall take place only on one of the following conditions

(a) the data subject has explicitly consented to the proposed transfer, after having been informed of the possible risks of such transfers due to the absence of an adequacy decision and appropriate safeguards;

(b) the transfer is necessary for the performance of a contract between the data subject and the controller or the implementation of pre-contractual measures taken at the data subject's request;

(c) the transfer is necessary for the conclusion or performance of a contract concluded in the interest of the data subject between the controller and another natural or legal person;

(d) the transfer is necessary for important reasons of public interest;

(e) the transfer is necessary for the establishment, exercise or defence of legal claims;

(f) the transfer is necessary to protect the vital interests of the data subject or of other persons, where the data subject is physically or legally incapable of giving consent.

Some comments on the Standard Contractual Clauses and Schrems II

In July 2020, the Court of Justice of the European Union (CJEU) in Case C-311/18 (*Data Protection Commissioner v Facebook Ireland Limited and Maximillian Schrems*; referred to as *Schrems II*) and Case C-623/17 (*Privacy International v Secretary of State for Foreign and Commonwealth Affairs and Others*) questioned the possibility of using the European Commission's Standard Contractual Clauses for transferring data to third countries (i.e. countries outside the EU or EEA). In this regard one of the most notable sections of the ruling is as follows:

> It is therefore, above all, for that controller or processor [i.e. the one undertaking the transfer] to verify, on a case-by-case basis and, where appropriate, in collaboration with the recipient of the data, whether the law of the third country of destination ensures adequate protection, under EU law, of personal data transferred pursuant to standard data protection clauses, by providing, where necessary, additional safeguards to those offered by those clauses.[24]

According to the ruling, it is no longer enough to just implement the Standard Contractual Clauses in order to transfer personal data to third countries. The exporter must also assess the country itself and its laws. This means that countries with unrestricted or far-reaching surveillance laws may be assessed as countries to which personal data cannot be transferred regardless of legal basis, unless

---

[24] Case C-311/18 *Data Protection Commissioner v Facebook Ireland Limited and Maximillian Schrems* [2020] ECLI:EU:C:2020:559. See also C-623/17 *Privacy International v Secretary of State for Foreign and Commonwealth Affairs and Others* [2020] ECLI:EU:C:2020:790.

additional safeguards are put in place. Such safeguards must be assessed on a case-by-case basis, but one option may be encryption if the exporter holds the key.

DPO's tips

- Perform a basic due diligence assessment on all existing processors. Start with business-critical suppliers.

- Create an easy process for assessing potential service providers with the help of your organisation's procurers. For example, include questions on at least the following areas:

  - Does the provider's national legislation provide appropriate safeguards on personal data equivalent to those of the EU or EEA?

  - Does the provider adhere to any security standards, for example ISO 27001?

  - Will the provider accept your template data protection agreement?

  - Does the provider at all times have an up-to-date list of sub-processors?

  - What are the default security and data protection settings, and how flexible is the system in terms of adaptation?

- It is not only a legal requirement to keep track of the legal mechanisms your organisation uses for third country transfers but it is also very good practice for business reasons. You might remember the Safe Harbor scheme, which in October 2015 was invalidated by the CJEU and led to the introduction of the Privacy Shield in August 2016. A lot of transfers were done based on Safe Harbor and when it was invalidated all companies had to quickly identify those transfers so that their mechanisms could be updated. The same could happen to any transfer mechanism.

MANAGING THE RIGHTS OF DATA SUBJECTS

One of the main reasons the Data Protection Directive was replaced with the GDPR was to strengthen the role of data subjects and make the data protection legislation more user-centric. The idea behind giving data subjects rights is to equip them with a mechanism to control the processing of their personal data. Even though data subjects had rights according to the directive, the rights were rarely used and they were, at least in some parts, vague. The GDPR clarified and elaborated the obligations of controllers on how to fulfil these rights. The rights are instrumental to achieving a broad picture of compliance, with 'investigations' done by the data subjects themselves. It would never be possible for the data protection authorities to investigate all controllers and processors. But everyone can control their personal data and act as mini data protection authorities by exercising their rights.

Balance of individuals' rights and controller's rights

Even though the rights of data subjects are at the very centre of the GDPR, they are not absolute rights. Businesses also have certain rights under EU legislation. The EU Charter of Fundamental Rights (not to be confused with the European Convention on Human Rights) applies to EU institutions and member states, and it grants rights to individuals[25] as well as to businesses. The principle on the fundamental right to conduct business (Article 16[26]) and the principle on the right to

---

25 Article 8 states the fundamental right to data protection.

26 Article 16 of the EU Charter of Fundamental Rights states the principle of the fundamental right to conduct a business. This article was referenced in the CJEU case *SABAM v Netlog*. The argument was made that a company has freedom to conduct its business in choosing which risk-mitigating measures to implement. The court stated, 'an injunction would result in a serious infringement of the freedom of [Netlog] to conduct its business since it would require [Netlog] to install a complicated and costly, permanent computer system at its own expense'. See C-360/10, *Belgische Vereniging van Auteurs, Componisten en Uitgevers CVBA (SABAM) v Netlog NV* [2012] ECLI:EU:C:2012:85 (https://eur-lex.europa.eu/legal-content/EN/TXT/PDF/?uri=CELEX:62010CJ0360_SUM&from=EN, p. 2).

property (Article 17[27]) have been interpreted by the CJEU and provide legal arguments for controllers (and processors) to push back on unreasonable broad data subject requests under applicable data protection legislation.

Right to information

From the data subjects' point of view, the right to information is vital to achieving the individual-centric perspective the GDPR is trying to establish. In the absence of clear and transparent information, it is not possible to revert the decision-making power to individuals. Individuals must receive the information they need to make a fact-based, conscious decision regarding the processing of their personal data. In this sense, the right to information is a prerequisite for all other data subject rights.

Consequently, the GDPR states that controllers should take appropriate measures to provide information about data processing to data subjects in a concise, transparent, intelligible and easily accessible form, using clear and plain language. This implies that controllers should refrain from using complicated legal terms or technical descriptions. In some circumstances, this imposes great challenges, as services delivered or offered to consumers are becoming more and more advanced. For example, it can be very hard to explain in simple terms how algorithms or artificial intelligence work – a challenge not always recognised by the regulators.

In summary, the information that controllers must give to data subjects is as follows:[28]

- information about the controller, such as name, registration number and contact details;

---

27 Article 17 was argued in the CJEU *Bayer* case to prevent the disclosure of trade secrets. In the actual case, such legal argumentation was found to be unsuccessful, but it was weighed against strong environmental concerns. It is likely that in a DSAR scenario, Article 17 will prevail and allow the controller to limit the disclosure of trade-secret-related personal data. See C-442/14, *Bayer CropScience SA-NV and Stichting De Bijenstichting v College voor de toelating van gewasbeschermingsmiddelen en biociden* [2016] ECLI:EU:C:2016:890.

28 The list is based on Article 13 of the GDPR.

- name and contact details of the controller's data protection officer (normally an email address is sufficient);

- a list of all the purposes of the data processing, accompanied by the legal basis for each purpose;

- a clear statement that some of the processing is based on the legal basis of legitimate interest and details of what that interest is (if applicable);

- details of who the controller transfers data to (legally called 'recipients') – it is enough to state the categories (i.e. the types) of the recipients;

- whether or not the controller will transfer the data outside the EU;

- either the exact retention period or how the retention period is calculated;

- the rights of the data subjects – for example, rectification, erasure and withdrawal of consent;

- a statement of the right to file a complaint with the data protection authority (a good practice is to also include the contact details of the relevant authority);

- a declaration of any automated decision-making, including profiling, and how this works and the consequences of such processing for the data subject.

Under normal circumstances, this information is given in a data protection notice[29] (often called a 'privacy notice'). It is best practice to design your privacy notice according to the 'layered' approach, which is intended to ensure the terms are presented in an easily readable format and with a clear overview.[30]

---

[29] Please note that it should not be referred to as a 'policy'. Policies are part of the internal governance structure.

[30] Article 29 Working Party (2017), *Guidelines on Transparency under Regulation 2016/679*, Directorate C of the European Commission, https://ec.europa.eu/newsroom/article29/item-detail.cfm?item_id=622227, p 19.

A privacy notice generally consists of three layers:

1. summarised highlights of the content;
2. the actual text;
3. a user-friendly section of frequently asked questions.

Note that you must present data subjects with all relevant information in such a way that they can access it with just a few clicks; fragmented information is not sufficient. Google was sanctioned by the CNIL in 2019 for presenting its policies across more than five clicks/layers, which was found to be a violation of Article 12 (transparency) and Article 13 (information).[31] The US Federal Trade Commission has used this approach to presenting privacy policies since 2012[32] and the method is also championed by the WP29 in guidelines issued in 2017.[33]

When reviewing the content of your data protection notice, you should consider:

- purpose of processing;
- scope;
- comprehensive declaration of data subjects' rights;
- factual statements of applicable information security practices;
- what data is used;

---

[31] 'Délibération SAN-2019-001' (2019), Commission Nationale de l'Informatique et des Libertés, https://www.legifrance.gouv.fr/affichCnil.do?oldAction=rechExpCnil&id=CN ILTEXT000038032552&fastReqId=2103387945&fastPos=1.

[32] 'FTC Issues Final Commission Report on Protecting Consumer Privacy' (2012), Federal Trade Commission, 26 March, https://www.ftc.gov/news-events/ press-releases/2012/03/ftc-issues-final-commission-report-protecting-consumer-privacy.

[33] Article 29 Working Party (2017), *Guidelines on Transparency under Regulation 2016/679*, Directorate C of the European Commission, https://ec.europa.eu/ newsroom/article29/item-detail.cfm?item_id=622227, pp. 8, 11, 14.

- why the data is used (specify the purpose and legal basis);
- how the data is used – considering primary services (e.g. customer transactions) and secondary services (e.g. security and to facilitate distribution);
- how and to whom data is disclosed;
- disclosure of third-party sub-processors used;
- contact details, including yours as the DPO;[34]
- change history.

You should also keep the seven principles in Article 5 of the GDPR (lawfulness, fairness and transparency; purpose limitation; data minimisation; accuracy; storage limitation; integrity and confidentiality; and accountability – see Chapter 1) in mind when you review the notice and make sure nothing in the notice contradicts these principles.

It is also important to review the process for updating the notice and how updates are communicated. First of all, you should make sure your organisation specifies the date of the latest update and check that all older versions are archived and saved for the future. Your organisation should also have a specified process for how data subjects are made aware of any updates.

Providing information in a transparent manner while safeguarding any sensitive commercial interests is a delicate balancing act. You should seek the expert advice of experienced privacy lawyers to ensure the quality of the text as well as to learn about any valuable approaches you can use.

---

34 Several regulators, among them the Swedish Datainspektionen, in early 2019 advertised that they would be making the issue of spelling out the DPO's name and contact information subject to proactive inquisitions.

Right to access

The right to access (also called a 'data subject access request' or DSAR) is the right of data subjects to ask for and receive certain information on request from the controller. The right to access is twofold. Firstly, data subjects have the right to obtain **confirmation** as to whether or not a controller is processing personal data about them (yes or no). Secondly, if the controller is processing data about a data subject, the data subject has the right to obtain **information** about that processing. The data subject also has the right to obtain a copy of the information that the controller is processing.

The list of information that controllers must give to data subjects is quite extensive, and controllers must establish processes and procedures to be able to deliver all of the required information. If an organisation holds a vast amount of data on each individual, a layered approach is in many circumstances most suitable. This means that the controller in the first instance gives all the basic data, excluding details that might not be of very much interest to the data subject, but states in the transcript that the data subject may request the full details. This could be applied, for example, for web traffic monitoring or session log files.

A controller usually has one month to respond to a DSAR. However, for complex requests or in the case of a high volume of requests, the time can be extended by a further two months.

Data subjects are usually required to provide proof of their identity before their data is released. A rule of thumb is that the time frame of one month starts when the organisation receives the DSAR but is suspended between the controller's request for proof of identity and when it is received.

Data subjects are entitled to make repetitive DSARs and controllers are normally obliged to respond to each one. However, a practical approach could be to provide the full transcript up to the date of the delivery of the first request, and then for any subsequent requests limit the transcripts to data collected since the previous request. If repetitive requests are manifestly unfounded or excessive, a controller may even refuse to respond or charge a reasonable fee (see Article 12 of the GDPR). The fee must be based on the actual administrative cost.

It should also be noted that the right to access can under rare circumstances be overruled by national legislation (e.g. this can be the case for medical records). However, this exception is very narrow.

Since controllers are responsible for ensuring that transcripts are only handed out to the data subjects to which they relate, controllers are not required to accept requests sent in via third-party suppliers if the identity of the data subject making the DSAR cannot be verified.

Right to rectification

If a data subject discovers that some information a controller is processing is wrong, they have the right to request and obtain rectification of the data. If a data subject discovers that some information is missing, they have the right to have the incomplete data completed. Thus, the right to rectification is about the data being both correct and complete.

A controller must execute a request for rectification without undue delay, but no later than one month following receipt of the request, or no later than one month following receipt of any information requested to confirm the requester's identity. The time period can in complex cases be extended by a further two months, but in these cases the individual should be informed of the extension within one month.

Right to erasure

The right to erasure, or as it is more often called the 'right to be forgotten', is probably the most well-known right in the GDPR, but at the same time also the most misunderstood right. It became famous among the public in May 2014, following the decision by the CJEU in the so-called *Google Spain* case.[35] This case established a right to have search results in search engines deleted under some circumstances, although it did not establish a right to have the original source of the data deleted. In this case, the original web article was allowed, but the court specified that it should no longer be findable via a search engine (Google). The right to have search results deleted is only valid within the EU and the search engine does not have to delete the links from its webpages elsewhere in the world.[36]

The right to erasure is now codified in Article 17 of the GDPR. According to the article, data subjects have the right to get their data deleted without undue delay if the prerequisites listed in the article are fulfilled. The right can be based on any of the criteria, so only one needs to be fulfilled. Following is a summary of the criteria:

- If the personal data is no longer necessary to pursue or fulfil the purposes for which it was collected and/or processed, it should be deleted on request. (In fact, it should probably already have been deleted.)

- If a data subject withdraws their consent where consent is the legal basis for processing and the controller cannot base the processing on any other legal basis, the data must be deleted.

---

[35] Case C-131/12 *Google Spain SL and Google Inc. v Agencia Española de Protección de Datos (AEPD) and Mario Costeja González* [2014] ECLI:EU:C:2014:317.

[36] Case C-507/17 *Google LLC, successor in law to Google Inc. v Commission nationale de l'informatique et des libertés (CNIL)* [2019] ECLI:EU:C:2019:772

- If a data subject objects to some processing where legitimate interest is the legal basis and the controller does not have an overriding legitimate ground to continue the processing, the data must be deleted.

- If the personal data is unlawfully processed, it must be deleted.

However, if a controller is processing data on the legal basis of fulfilment of a contract or as a legal obligation, these circumstances will prevail over the right to erasure. Thus, when it is acting as a controller, your organisation must have clear records on the legal basis for every processing activity. Otherwise, you will not be able to demonstrate compliance concerning requests for erasure.

The same stipulations regarding the time limit apply here as apply to the right to rectification.

Right to restriction of processing

In addition to the rights to erasure and rectification, data subjects also have a right to require controllers to restrict processing under some circumstances. If the requirements are met, the controller must temporarily limit the processing. According to Article 18 of the GDPR, this right can be exercised in four different scenarios:

- If the data subject questions the accuracy of the personal data. During the period of time required to verify the data, the data subject may request that the data is not processed (i.e. restricted).

- If some processing is found to be unlawful, the data subject can, instead of asking for the data to be deleted, request the controller to restrict the processing.

- If it is established that the controller no longer needs some specific personal data, the data subject can require the controller to keep the data during the establishment, exercise and defence of legal claims.

- If the data subject has objected to processing that is done on the legal basis of legitimate interest, the controller can be requested to temporarily restrict the processing during the investigation period (i.e. when the controller is assessing whether the legitimate grounds of the controller override those of the data subject).

During the period of restriction, the controller may only store the data. When the restriction is about to be lifted, the data subject must be informed.

From the controller's perspective, the right to restriction can be quite tricky to manage since most IT systems are built without such functionality in place. Going forward, the functionality to restrict should, if necessary, be included in the list of system requirements.

Again, the same time limits apply as are listed above for the rights of rectification and erasure.

Right to data portability

One of the brand new rights assigned to data subjects in the GDPR is the right to portability. This right immediately became a buzzword in 2012 following the European Commission's publication of the first draft of the GDPR. It allows data subjects to receive the personal data that they have provided to a controller in a structured, commonly used and machine-readable format. However, the right to portability has some major restrictions:

- It only applies to processing based on consent or contract.

- It only applies to personal data provided by a data subject.

- The controller may use any format that meets the requirement to provide the information in a structured, commonly used and machine-readable format. There is no standard for this.[37]

---

37 The European Commission encourages data controllers to ensure the interoperability of the data format provided; see Article 29 Working Party (2017), *Guidelines on the Right to Data Portability*, Directorate C of the European Commission, https://ec.europa.eu/newsroom/article29/item-detail.cfm?item_id=611233, p. 3.

Categories of data indicated by the WP29 to be 'provided by the data subject'[38]

- Data actively and knowingly provided by a data subject (e.g. mailing address, username or age).

- Observational data provided by a data subject by virtue of the use of a service or device. This may, for example, include the person's search history, traffic data and location data. It may also include other raw data, such as the heartbeat tracked by a wearable device.

The right to portability is not only regulated by the GDPR. For example, the regulation known as PSD2 – which relates to payments – also includes a right to portability.[39] You will need to know which laws and regulations apply to your organisation.

The major difference between the right to access and the right to portability is that the latter gives data subjects a right to receive data from one controller so they can transfer it to another controller for further processing. A key aspect of the right to portability is that a controller that answers a data portability request is not responsible for any further processing by the data subject or by another company that receives the personal data. The original controller does not need to consider whether the receiving party will process the transmitted personal data in line with data protection law. Another interesting aspect is that a controller does not need to retain data beyond the otherwise applicable retention periods simply to serve any potential future data portability request.

---

38 *Guidelines on the Right to 'Data Portability'* (2017), European Commission, https://ec.europa.eu/newsroom/article29/item-detail.cfm?item_id=611233.

39 'Directive (EU) 2015/2366 of the European Parliament and of the Council of 25 November 2015 on payment services in the internal market, amending Directives 2002/65/EC, 2009/110/EC and 2013/36/EU and Regulation (EU) No 1093/2010, and repealing Directive 2007/64/EC' (2015), European Parliament and European Council, https://eur-lex.europa.eu/legal-content/EN/TXT/?uri=CELEX:32015L2366.

A further aspect to emphasise is that the right to data portability has no effect on the other rights and obligations in the GDPR. For instance, data portability does not automatically trigger the erasure of the data from the systems of the data controller. Furthermore, a data subject can continue to use and benefit from the transmitting data controller's service even after a data portability operation.

Lastly, besides empowering data subjects, portability has an ideological purpose, since it facilitates switching between different service providers. By that means, it fosters the development of new services in the context of the EU's digital single market strategy,[40] and thus it encourages competition and supports the free flow of personal data within the EU. In light of this, it is somewhat strange that there is no requirement for the receiving controllers to accept and process personal data transmitted following a data portability request. It may even be that the receiving controller cannot legally process all of the received data, considering the basic principle that only personal data that is necessary and relevant for the receiving data controller to perform the service can be processed.

The same time limits as above apply upon receipt of a data portability request.

Right to object

A data subject's right to object to processing is very limited. Such a request can only be made if the legal ground for processing is:

- that the processing is necessary for the performance of a task carried out in the public interest; or

- that the processing is in the legitimate interest of the controller.

---

40 'A digital single market strategy for Europe' (2014), European Commission, https://eur-lex.europa.eu/legal-content/EN/TXT/?uri=celex%3A52015DC0192.

Even in these cases, the right to object is not absolute. The controller might be able to demonstrate compelling legitimate grounds for the processing that override the interests, rights and freedoms of the data subject. This requires the controller to conduct a balancing test upon receipt of an objection from a data subject. The balancing test should be based on the particular situation relating to the specific data subject – and, for obvious reasons, it should not be a duplicate of the first balancing test in the legitimate interests assessment (LIA). Rather, it should be an even more thorough examination of all the relevant circumstances, and only if the data controller can find **compelling legitimate grounds** may the processing continue.

Make sure you understand the difference between a data subject revoking previously given consent and a data subject objecting to processing. For information on unsubscribes from email marketing, see the section 'Processing of personal data for marketing purposes' below.

Once again, the same time limits apply upon receipt of a request.

AUTOMATED INDIVIDUAL DECISION-MAKING, INCLUDING PROFILING

During the past decade, the means of analysing data have exploded. At the time of writing, the trend towards introducing artificial intelligence (AI) and machine learning into all sorts of business is very strong. AI, like other similar techniques for data-mining and working with big data, is centred on collecting and analysing data. If AI is applied to personal data, it is possible to draw deep conclusions about a person on the individual level. Theoretically, some companies could even know more about you than you do yourself. But, just like humans, computers can draw the wrong conclusions and be biased and narrow minded – particularly if the data being used is wrong. All of this can have severe effects on individuals, not least if some important decisions are made automatically. For example, if you apply for a mortgage and the relevant data has not been updated with your new seven-figure salary, your online application may be instantly denied.

To decrease the likelihood of a negative impact on individuals, Article 22 of the GDPR contains a right for data subjects not to be subject to decisions based **solely** on automated processing if the decision would have a legal effect (or any other significant effect) on the data subject. However, since automation can be both efficient and in the common interest, there are some exceptions to the prohibition. Automated individual decision-making is allowed:

- if it is necessary to enter into or perform a contract between the data subject and the controller; or

- if the data subject has given their explicit consent.

However, the controller must implement suitable measures to safeguard the data subject's rights and legitimate interests. At a minimum, the controller must implement the possibility for the data subject to obtain human intervention in the controller's processing, and allow the data subject to express their point of view and to contest the automated decision.

A common practice in online loan applications is for banks to use automated means to approve or deny a loan by letting a computer analyse the applicant's data and make a decision. For banks to be compliant, they need to have a process in place for human intervention and the ability for the applicant to contest the decision.

Furthermore, there are specific information requirements if a controller uses either automated decision-making or profiling. In those cases, the controller must give meaningful information about the logic involved, as well as the significance and the envisaged consequences of such processing for the data subject. How detailed the information should be must be assessed on a case-by-case basis. It is within your tasks as the DPO to assess the information and report on any non-compliance to the controller.

DPO's tips

- The most visible part of your organisation's data protection work is the external privacy notice. Making sure you have an excellent privacy notice is an easy way to avoid problems and spare yourself a lot of questions from your customers.

- Evaluate and improve the various processes you use around individuals' exercise of their rights, but don't forget about return on investment. If the number of requests is low, it most likely won't make sense to purchase the most advanced IT solutions. It may be both more efficient and cheaper to have a manual process.

PROCESSING OF PERSONAL DATA FOR MARKETING PURPOSES

During the past decade, the so-called adtech industry has evolved into a multi-billion-dollar market. Most of the big social media platforms – for example, Facebook and LinkedIn – are more or less entirely based on revenue from ads and other forms of marketing. 'Marketing' is a very broad term, however. It can be divided into two categories: 'direct marketing' and 'mass marketing'. In this book, we use 'direct marketing' for marketing that targets a single individual and 'mass marketing' for everything else. It should be noted that both types of marketing can include the processing of personal data – for example, to analyse consumer behaviour. The split between the marketing types only relates to method of distribution.

Both direct marketing and mass marketing are surrounded by various laws; from the data protection perspective, the ePrivacy Directive and the GDPR are the most important. While the GDPR is general, the ePrivacy Directive is a more detailed piece of legislation on the electronic communications sector. For a more in-depth review of the interplay between the ePrivacy Directive and the GDPR, we highly recommend *Opinion 5/2019* of the EDPB.[41]

Direct marketing

Direct marketing includes a range of distribution channels, such as email marketing, push notifications and paper letters. Some of these are regulated by the ePrivacy Directive while others are not. Common to all of them is that the processing of personal data for direct marketing purposes may be regarded as being carried out on the basis of legitimate interest, according to Recital 47 of the GDPR. Hence, all such processing must be preceded by a LIA (see the section on legitimate interest in Chapter 1). However, a data subject always has the right to object to the processing of personal data for direct marketing purposes, according to Articles 21(2) and 21(3) of the GDPR.

Mass marketing

Mass marketing includes banner ads, ads on public transport, TV commercials and many more things. For most, or even all, mass marketing campaigns to be efficient, their ads must appear in the right places and at the right times to catch their intended audience. Therefore, an organisation that uses mass marketing must know its customers or users. This knowledge is gained by analysing the behaviour and customs of the consumers. Personal data will be the basis for these analyses, but it should as far as possible be either anonymised data or at least pseudonymised data. The challenge here is that the mere number of data points on each individual may, in reality, make individuals identifiable.

Most organisations will probably rely on legitimate interest as the legal basis for all processing of personal data for mass

---

41 See *Opinion 5/2019 on the Interplay between the ePrivacy Directive and the GDPR, in Particular Regarding the Competence, Tasks and Powers of Data Protection Authorities* (2019), European Data Protection Board, https://edpb.europa.eu/sites/edpb/files/files/file1/201905_edpb_opinion_eprivacydir_gdpr_interplay_en_0.pdf.

marketing. But, just as for direct marketing, the legitimate interest of the controller to process data for marketing purposes can never outweigh an objection from a data subject.

PROCESSING OF EMPLOYEES' PERSONAL DATA

The processing of personal data within an HR department will usually be done for several different purposes, such as sourcing of candidates, rehabilitation of employees, salary payments and annual evaluations. Several different legal bases will also be applicable. This section looks at the most common processing activities relating to the employee journey: recruitment, either by active applications or by sourcing; administration of the ongoing employment; and termination of the employment, either by the employer or by the employee. Each stage consists of various purposes as well as various legal bases.

Recruitment

In recruitment, it is important to distinguish between individuals who actively apply for an open position and sourced candidates that the organisation, or a recruitment agency, finds and contacts.

Applicants

The application process typically begins with the organisation posting a job ad and giving applicants instructions on how to apply for the open position. Since the aim of this process is to enter into an employment agreement, the personal data processing required for this stage could be seen as necessary in order to take steps at the request of the data subject prior to entering into a contract. But some specific steps within the process may have other legal bases – for example, if there are legal requirements for physical tests.

After the recruitment has been finalised, the organisation may save relevant data on all candidates in order to defend itself against legal claims – for example, claims from a candidate who feels that they have been discriminated against. The retention period should be the same as the time period for filing claims.

The hiring organisation may also ask for consent from applicants to keep their data for the purpose of reaching out with details of future openings. If consent is given, the organisation can store and use the personal data for this purpose for the time period the candidate has given consent for.

Sourcing of candidates

Sourcing of candidates – that is, when an organisation searches for and contacts candidates – is slightly more complicated. An organisation cannot rely on the processing being necessary in order to take steps at the request of the data subject prior to entering into a contract. This is simply because a candidate sourced in this way does not know about the processing. For the same reason, consent is not possible. Instead, the organisation may rely on legitimate interest. But it is important to remember that the requirements around giving out information are the same for sourced candidates as they are for other applicants. This includes limits on when information must be given.

The rules around saving candidates' data for future use are the same as those for applicants.

Background checks

Before a candidate is hired, one of the last steps most organisations do is a background check. This may be more or less intrusive depending on the industry. The legal basis can also vary. In some industries and for certain positions, a background check can be a legal requirement. For example, that is the case for most positions in the military and for certain positions in the financial industry.

If a background check is done as a legal requirement, the processing of personal data can be grounded on this basis.

Processing during the employment relationship

An employer may process the personal data of its employees for many reasons. Normal purposes include anything from issuing key cards to vacation planning. Just as for any other processing, all the requirements and obligations in the GDPR must be fulfilled, but there may also be specific labour laws that it is necessary to comply with. Table 3.1 lists the most common purposes and the legal basis that is usually used for each purpose.

Table 3.1 Legal bases for personal data processing for various purposes within HR

Purpose	Legal basis
Manage, plan and organise employees	Contractual obligation
Pay salary to employees	Contractual obligation
Evaluate employees	Legitimate interest
Manage equality and diversity in the workplace	Legal obligation (potentially also legitimate interest)
Administer health in the workplace	Legal obligation or contractual obligation
Promote enjoyment and pleasure in the workplace (project kick-offs, celebrations on birthdays, etc.)	Legitimate interest
Deliver and administer rights and benefits related to employment	Contractual obligation
Administer employee expenses	Contractual obligation
Administer access management	Legitimate interest or legal obligation

(Continued)

Table 3.1 (Continued)

Purpose	Legal basis
Provide an entrance control system	Legitimate interest (potentially also legal obligation)
Provide closed-circuit television (CCTV)	Legitimate interest
Prevent data loss	Legitimate interest
Monitor IT system usage	Legitimate interest
Post employee photos on the company intranet	Consent

As the table indicates, the possibility of using consent as the legal basis for processing employee personal data is very limited and it should probably be avoided if possible.

Processing after the employment ends

Employment can end by various means – the employee may quit, the employee may retire, the employee may be dismissed and so on. Depending on the reason for the end of the employment, the employer may keep and continue to process the former employee's personal data for various purposes. Just like during the employment relationship, the legal bases may vary by purpose. Table 3.2 outlines the most common purposes and their legal bases.

DPO's tips

- It is in most cases not possible to rely on consent as the legal basis for processing employee personal data.
- Make sure you assess and apply proper retention times.

- If a candidate or employee raises a DSAR, it is debated whether notes from references and interviews should be included in the transcript or not. On the one hand, these normally contain personal data relating to the candidate or employee but, on the other hand, because they contain the opinions of the reference writer or interviewer, they also constitute personal data of those individuals. There is no clear best practice in these cases, but each organisation should at least make an assessment of whether or not to include such data in DSARs.

Table 3.2 Legal bases for processing of personal data for various purposes after employment has ended

Purpose	Legal basis
Defend the organisation against legal claims	Legitimate interest
Support the former employee with information	Legitimate interest
Pension and tax reasons	Legal obligation

MANAGING DATA PROTECTION INCIDENTS

One of the new features in the GDPR is the obligation to report personal data breaches to the authorities and data subjects. Similar requirements were earlier deployed in most states in the USA, although they mainly focused on general security breaches rather than personal data.

As the DPO, you will play a crucial role in assessing personal data incidents, but it is always ultimately the organisation that makes all decisions. The DPO can make suggestions but not decisions, as that would be a conflict of interest.

We recommend that you include yourself in the communication flows around the incident response, but we would suggest caution about getting closely involved in the practicalities, since this can be time-consuming and time sensitive. Make sure that you have ensured the quality of the data breach incident process and that you are seen as a point of escalation for more complex decisions. Typically, the DPO is part of a task force that receives suggestions for action, where the DPO can weigh in if it is deemed necessary. We would advise you to get hands-on only in the most complex or sensitive cases.

Internal incident reporting

We have previously stressed the importance of training and awareness-raising among people in your organisation. Training must include clear information on what a personal data incident is and how to report a suspected incident. Unless it is clear to everyone what a personal data incident is and the importance of reporting them, your organisation will ultimately fail in its long-term proactive data protection work.

The threshold for reporting suspected breaches should be as low as possible to ensure that all breaches are caught. In most organisations, this means that some reported incidents will not be considered personal data breaches following assessment. It is important to keep a register of all reported incidents and the assessments of each – even the incidents that are not ultimately deemed to be personal data breaches. If you are audited, your organisation should be able to show all assessments to the regulator so it can evaluate whether the assessments were correct or not.

Assessing the incident

Most organisations experience incidents regularly, whether from a power-out, an employee stumbling over a cable or the loss of a smartphone containing the addresses of all suppliers. Only a fraction of all incidents will concern personal data, and only some of the incidents concerning personal data will also constitute personal data breaches. The remainder of this section examines when an incident should be classified as a personal data breach and looks at the DPO's role in incident reporting.

It is far better to have done assessments and come to the 'wrong' conclusion than not to have done any assessments at all. Furthermore, make sure that each assessment includes a proper evaluation of each identified risk.

When is an incident a personal data breach?

In the context of the GDPR, a personal data breach is defined as 'a breach of security leading to the accidental or unlawful destruction, loss, alteration, unauthorised disclosure of, or access to, personal data transmitted, stored or otherwise processed' (Article 4). Broken down, this definition consists of two distinct premises:

- a breach of security that
- causes any of the listed harms to an individual.

Thus, some events that have a negative impact on individuals do not constitute a personal data breach, even though they are breaches of provisions in the GDPR, such as processing for new purposes in breach of the original purpose. On the other hand, if someone with legitimate access to a database out of curiosity looks at their neighbour's record, it is considered a personal data breach since it is unauthorised access.

At times, it may not be clear whether an incident constitutes a personal data breach or not. When evaluating whether an incident is or is not a personal data breach, it can be useful to think about the reasons behind the introduction of this idea in the GDPR. According to Recital 85, a personal data breach can, if not addressed in a timely and appropriate manner, result in any of a number of negative impacts on individuals, such as physical damage (e.g. bodily harm), material damage (e.g. fraud) or non-material damage (e.g. reputation).

Reporting to supervisory authorities

In the previous section, we emphasised the importance of having very efficient and effective internal incident reporting, to enable the organisation to quickly assemble the relevant information, assess the incident and report it internally. Just as importantly, the organisation should have processes and templates for reporting personal data breaches to the supervisory authority – not least since incidents have an unfortunate habit of occurring the day before Christmas or in the middle of summer vacation. Incidents must be reported within 72 hours, and this time will feel very short if you are not prepared and don't know what to do. In this section, we will examine when and how to do this efficiently.

When should a personal data breach be reported to the supervisory authority?

Formally, only confirmed personal data breaches must be reported to the supervisory authority. On the other hand, it may take some time to assess and confirm whether or not an incident is a personal data breach. For this reason, a controller or processor has some time to assess an incident before the 72-hour clock starts ticking. Once an incident has been confirmed to be a personal data breach, it must be reported to the supervisory authority without undue delay, and never later than 72 hours. The initial investigation phase should be kept short and if it is not possible to confirm whether or not an incident is a personal data breach within a few days, it is probably good practice to send in a notification with an explanation about the ongoing investigation. It is possible to later either add more context and details of the circumstances or withdraw a personal data breach notification.

If a controller or processor for any reason misses the deadline of 72 hours, they must state the reasons for the delay when they do eventually send in their notification.

One very important exception applies to an incident that constitutes a personal data breach per se but that is unlikely to result in a risk to the rights or freedoms of data subjects. In such cases, the breach does not need to be reported.

What should be reported?

If a controller has established that a personal data breach has occurred, it must report at least the following information to the authority:[42]

- a description of the personal data breach – that is, what happened (e.g. an email with a bank statement has been sent to the wrong recipient);

- the categories of data subjects concerned (e.g. bank customers);

- the approximate number of data subjects concerned (e.g. two people);

- the categories and approximate number of personal data records concerned (e.g. one bank statement);

- the names and contact details of the DPO and/or other relevant contact points (e.g. name, email and phone number);

- the likely consequences of the personal data breach (e.g. a person will see the bank statement of another person);

- a description of the measures taken or proposed to address the personal data breach, including, where appropriate, measures to mitigate its possible adverse effects (e.g. both customers have individually been contacted about what has happened and the receiving customer has declared they have deleted the email).

How do you report a breach?

Most data protection authorities have standardised forms for reporting breaches. Some even have online tools. In the UK, you also have the option to call in a breach during normal business hours.[43]

---

42 The content of this list (except for the examples) is taken from Article 33 of the GDPR.

43 See 'Data breach reporting' (n.d.), Information Commissioner's Office, https://ico.org.uk/for-organisations/report-a-breach/personal-data-breach.

Note that freedom of information applies to documents held by a public authority. Do not hand in company sensitive information, or, if you decide that you must include such information, make sure you include a request for confidentiality.

Notifying data subjects

First and foremost, your organisation should distinguish between when it is mandatory to notify data subjects of a breach and when it is good business practice to do so. These are two very different things. The first mostly concerns being compliant, while the second mostly concerns the organisation's reputation. As the public is becoming more and more aware of privacy issues, striking this balance will become increasingly important. History has taught us that most large security breaches sooner or later become public, even if no specific individual was subject to a high risk of harm.

Strictly speaking, legally a controller should inform data subjects of a personal data breach, without undue delay, if the breach is likely to result in a high risk to them. The content of the information to provide is outlined in Article 34 of the GDPR.

However, if the controller has taken mitigating actions such that the risk to the data subjects in reality is no longer high and is unlikely to materialise, there is no obligation to inform the data subjects.

DPO's tips

- It is commonly said that it is not a question of **if** but **when** your organisation will have a personal data breach. As this statement is probably true, it is a good idea to test your processes a couple of times through 'dry runs'. You will probably discover that some parts that looked good in theory are not as good in practice. This might be a time-consuming task, but it will save you and your organisation a lot of stress when a real breach happens and the 72 hours start ticking.

- Keep in mind that the submission of a personal data breach to the supervisory authority may not be protected by confidentiality. Most member states in the EU follow the principle of freedom of information and access to public documents, which allows the public access to information held by public authorities.

- Be careful how you word your submission and choose a secure file transfer system when you send it to the authority.

- For most people, 'privacy-enhancing technologies' (PETs) is unknown terminology. It can be a good idea to include a few examples in your internal data protection policy (see earlier in this chapter).

SUMMARY

In this chapter, we have discussed the various data protection processes an organisation must implement to be compliant with the GDPR – for example, how to manage the various rights of data subjects. The chapter also covered the controller's responsibilities, such as implementing a ROPA and procedures for ensuring data protection by design.

Lastly, the chapter explained the basics of how to assess and contractually bind processors, what a personal data breach is and when a controller must report it to the authorities.

4 UNDERSTANDING RISK

At this stage, it should be apparent that almost all implementations of the requirements and obligations in the General Data Protection Regulation (GDPR) should be done in a risk-based manner. Bearing that in mind, it is no wonder that the word 'risk' is mentioned around 75 times throughout the text. As a consequence, a huge responsibility is put on organisations that intend to process personal data. Most implementations will need case-by-case assessments of the different forms of risk. As the data protection officer (DPO), you will in one form or another be involved in many risk assessments; thus, you should know what a risk is in the context of the GDPR as well as what definition of risk is used in other circumstances – for example, by IT security or management.

First of all, the main form of risk that the GDPR is concerned with is risks to individuals due to the processing of personal data. Let's call these 'data protection risks'.[1] These are threats to individuals. It is important to assess the likelihood of these threats materialising, understand what the impact would be if that happened and plan how to mitigate the impact if necessary.

However, data protection risks thus defined are not the same thing as what your risk department will usually call risks, and thus data protection risks will not be assessed or calculated by them. What they are concerned with is business risks –

---

1   They are also often referred to as 'privacy risks'.

that is, what risks the business is exposed to. Data protection risks and business risks can be (and often are) related, but you cannot assume your risk department can assess data protection risks and translate them into business risks. They will probably need your help with this. Highlighting risks in your management reports will be one of the most important aspects of your internal monitoring and reporting work.

Sometimes a third category of risks is added. We can call these 'compliance risks'. Compliance risks relate to the likelihood and impact of not being compliant – that is, breaking the law. It is important to separate these from data protection risks since not all non-compliance implies a data protection risk. Normally the two are the same – for example, not having appropriate security constitutes a breach of Articles 5(1)(f) and 32 of the GDPR (i.e. compliance risk) but it also exposes data subjects to a data protection risk. On top of that, non-compliance also exposes an organisation to business risk in the form of fines or a bad reputation.

This chapter first looks at the basics of how risk is calculated and then considers each of three types of risk in turn.

THE BASICS OF CALCULATING RISK

Regardless of what type of risk you are dealing with, the basic formula is always the same:

Risk = likelihood of event happening × impact if event happens

For example, you want to know what the risk is of a power outage occurring in your data centre (the event). Asking this question will immediately prompt many people to start thinking about the impact and potential solutions, but impact is, as we stated above, only one of two elements in risk calculation. Solutions should be considered in a later step. First the likelihood should be estimated, and then the impact. The risk is then the product of the likelihood of a power outage occurring (not likely) and the impact (no service). In this case, there is a very low likelihood but a very high impact. Many organisations assign scores of 1 to 5 so they can perform the calculation above. In this case, the likelihood might be assigned a score of 1 and the impact a score of 5. Whether or not this is a risk your organisation is willing to accept depends on its risk appetite. It probably will not, in which case some form of mitigating action will be implemented (e.g. back-up power).

Risk appetite is the amount of risk an organisation is willing to take in different areas. It should consider both likelihood and impact. Sometimes an organisation can accept a large number of smaller likelihoods if the impact per incident would be low, but other organisations cannot.

At the opposite end of the spectrum, and probably harder to decide, there is the question of whether an organisation should accept high impacts with very low likelihoods. For almost all risks, there exists a point where lowering the likelihood of an event with very severe impact comes at a huge cost. This leads us to the next phase of risk calculation and risk management: how to treat identified risks.

How to treat identified risks

In risk management, there are normally deemed to be four ways of treating identified risks:

- **Avoid** the risk (i.e. don't engage in the activity or practice that generates the risk).

- **Mitigate** the risk – also called 'control the risk' (i.e. reduce the likelihood and/or the impact by introducing mitigating actions, such as changing a process).

- **Accept** the risk (this option is most attractive if both the likelihood and the impact are fairly low).

- **Transfer** the risk (i.e. let someone else take on the risk, such as by buying insurance).

Depending on the type of risk, one or more of these approaches might not be an option.

Residual risk

Another key concept to understand is residual risk. This is the risk that remains after the chosen treatment. That gives us the following formula:

Residual risk = Original risk [i.e. *likelihood × impact*] *– treatment of risk* [i.e. avoid, mitigate, accept or transfer]

It is vital to understand the difference between risk and residual risk since it affects whether or not a controller must consult the supervisory authority after conducting a data protection impact assessment (DPIA) (Article 36 of the GDPR). The risk as such should first be evaluated without considering mitigating actions. The residual risk is the risk still present after considering the already taken or planned mitigating actions. It can sometimes be challenging not to consider general mitigating activities that are already implemented that decrease the risk – for example, general firewalls or access management systems.

Another more practical challenge is that a risk can be mitigated by several activities of different sorts. Generally, these can be divided into three categories: people, process and technology. Each has different effects on risk and at different costs. The standard risk model as described above does not help you to choose what to do to maximise the mitigating effect and minimise the cost of mitigation.

At the end of each risk assessment, you should aim to have a clear table of risks and mitigating activities to help you assess what you should do. Table 4.1 provides an example using scales from 1 to 5 for both likelihood and impact.

DATA PROTECTION RISKS

From a GDPR perspective, a data protection risk arises from the processing of personal data that could lead to any of the following negative consequences for an individual (Recital 75):

163

- physical damage, such as bodily harm;

- material damage, such as loss of expensive items, destruction of property or fraud;

- non-material damage, such as discrimination, identity theft, damage to reputation or any other significant social disadvantage;

- deprivation of rights and freedoms;

- prevention from exercising control over one's own personal data.

Consequently, a data protection risk, according to the GDPR, is a broader concept than most would think since the impact does not need to cause harm in the way the word is normally used. As mentioned above, the mere fact that there is a risk of an individual experiencing a negative effect (e.g. being deprived of information) will constitute a data protection risk, even if the processing of the actual personal data itself is completely compliant. Another example could be if the access management at a company is not restricted to what each person needs to fulfil their work; that would constitute a risk since someone could accidentally see information about a person that they don't need to see.

Some examples of data protection risks to individuals include accidental or unlawful destruction, loss, alteration or unauthorised disclosure caused by inadequate security of the personal data. Another risk could be the use of personal data for unsanctioned purposes, caused by a lack of awareness among employees.

In Chapter 3 in the section on DPIAs, we saw that identifying the likelihood and severity of a data protection risk within a DPIA should be done with reference to the origin, nature, scope, context and purposes of the data processing. Depending on the circumstances, the same threat could have different impacts on different individuals and also require different mitigating actions. Such circumstances will create a challenge since risk should be evaluated based on an objective assessment.

Table 4.1 Results of a risk assessment

Description (the event)	Risk (likelihood, impact)	Mitigating action	Cost/resource of mitigating action	Residual risk	Accountable person	Comments
Transfer of data to a processor without a data processing agreement in place	3, 2	Change the process of onboarding vendors by introducing sign-off by the DPO	Less than 50 hours £0 (only DPO salary)	1, 2	Procurement director	Deadline for agreement of new process: 25 January

165

Whether or not it is even possible to conduct an objective risk assessment could be questioned, as it relates to how individuals perceive risks.

One way of demonstrating compliance regarding identification of the risks relating to a specific instance of processing could be to identify the best practices for mitigating those risks. Examples include adhering to approved codes of conduct, approved certifications, guidelines provided by the European Data Protection Board or even indications provided by you as the DPO (Recital 77 of the GDPR).

Calculating data protection risks

Article 35 of the GDPR states that a DPIA should be done before processing begins if it is likely to result in a high risk to the rights and freedoms of individuals. Thus, it is important for you to be able to calculate the potential impact of data protection risks. As previously stated, this should be assessed and evaluated in an objective way, considering the likelihood and severity (Recital 90) and with reference to the nature, scope, context and purposes of the data processing.

Some of the aspects that should be considered are:

- the number of data subjects (more data subjects equals higher risk);

- the type of personal data (more sensitive personal data equals higher risk);

- the amount of personal data about each data subject (more data on each data subject equals higher risk);

- the type of technology used (new, unproven or intrusive technology normally equals higher risk);

- how data subjects can exercise their rights (the more complicated, the higher risk);

- the age of the data subjects (younger equals higher risk);

- the duration of the processing (long retention time equals higher risk).

As mentioned above, even though the basic elements you need to consider when you assess data protection risks are fairly straightforward, in reality, assessing them objectively is normally very challenging. Just try to think objectively about the following: What constitutes a long duration? For how long is something considered to be new technology? What makes technology intrusive? And what is a large amount of data? Each of these is very contextual and subjective.

Another challenge is how to weigh up different aspects against each other – for example, the number of data subjects against the number of data points about each individual, or the number of data subjects against the sensitivity of the data. At first, such discussions might sound very theoretical, but they are not. Since resources are limited, everything you do must be prioritised. Should you first mitigate the risks of a processing activity concerning a few data subjects with sensitive data or large-scale processing of non-sensitive data? This comes down to philosophical questions on the nature of value – what has a value and how should it be calculated? Under normal circumstances, data sensitivity weighs more heavily than number of data subjects. But at some point, the two should intersect and the number should outweigh the sensitivity. But where?

Mitigating data protection risks

Mitigating data protection risks is mainly about how the mitigating actions will affect the risks to the data subjects. Putting yourself in the position of the data subjects is usually a good starting point for such an exercise. By doing so, you will soon understand that the four ways of treating a risk (avoid, mitigate, accept or transfer) are difficult – but not impossible – to apply to data protection risks.

You should also add a more subjective 'creepy test' – in other words, how will a data subject experience the effects of the processing or feel as a result of it? The normal first instinct is that you should always try to avoid data protection risks, but that is not necessarily true. In most cases, you should balance the negative impact on data protection and privacy against the benefits that data subjects will receive. Since almost all services do in one way or another include some form of personal data processing, it is important not to choose to 'avoid' at any price. The higher the benefit for the individual, the higher the risks the individual is likely to be willing to take. A challenge is that all people are different, and it is not clear from the GDPR whether you should consider each data protection risk from the viewpoint of an average person or the most sensitive person. Furthermore, the average person is very different from country to country.

Think of a health service that compares symptoms across patients on a global basis to enable more precise diagnoses. A person with a very rare disease whose current doctor cannot pinpoint what exact variant they have is likely to be more willing to share their health records with the service than another person whose doctor has correctly diagnosed them without the service. Hence, which person should you consider when doing a risk assessment? People are likely to be more inclined to take a big risk if the upside is great than if the personal gain is low.

This example shows that addressing data protection risks is not always about decreasing the risk to zero. It is more about balancing different aspects against each other and finding the point at which the various aspects are in the best possible alignment.

Lastly, it should be mentioned that Articles 5(1)f and 32 of the GDPR state that the security measures you implement should ensure an **appropriate** level of security. By 'appropriate', the legislator means that the controller should consider the state of the art of security measures and the costs of implementation of these in relation to the risks and the nature of the personal data, and also update the security measures as the processing changes over time.

COMPLIANCE RISKS

As stated above, a compliance risk is the risk of being non-compliant. It relates to all the requirements and obligations in the GDPR. Most of these correspond to the rights of data subjects and aim in one way or another to reinforce them. But not all of them do. Some requirements and obligations are aimed at making audits easier or other vital parts of the data protection system efficient. If a controller or processor does not abide by these, it is not certain whether the data protection risk for individuals will be increased,[2] regardless of the controller or processor being in breach of the GDPR.

Therefore, from a company and compliance perspective, these risks are just as important as other risks since they will in most cases correspond to business risks. However, from individuals' perspective, they are probably less important.

Calculating and mitigating compliance risks

Compliance is not binary; it's not as simple as being or not being compliant. Having a binary approach to compliance may lead to approaching it as a tick-box exercise, and that doesn't serve anyone.

Authorities will certainly look at whether an organisation has a breach plan, a record of processing activities (ROPA) and an appointed DPO. However, they will also investigate whether the breach plan is appropriate, whether the ROPA contains all the necessary data, and whether the DPO meets all the criteria and does not have any conflicting roles. Thus, organisations must go beyond just ticking boxes to ensure they have everything in place. They must have comprehensive documentation to prove that they have done the right assessments in setting up their breach plan, implementing their ROPA and appointing their DPO. Only by fulfilling all of these requirements can they mitigate compliance risks.

---

2   We should state that some will not agree with this position and will be of the opinion that every breach constitutes a privacy risk for data subjects.

There is a chance that even if an organisation fulfils all of these requirements, an authority might still find it in breach of the GDPR in some way. However, the risk of not being compliant or being hit by a severe sanction is far lower if everything is done correctly and proper documentation is in place.

BUSINESS RISKS

Most organisations already have a model for risk management, usually called enterprise risk management (ERM). An ERM normally consists of methods and processes aimed at managing risks and grasping opportunities relating to the organisation's business objectives. It is a way of systematically identifying events that might materialise and categorising them according to whether they might be good or bad in terms of achieving the business' objectives. All risks must be assessed in the same way within an organisation, otherwise management will not be able to compare the risks against each other to make informed decisions. As with data protection risks and compliance risks, business risks should be assessed in terms of likelihood and impact. But the ERM should also include a way of mitigating risks and monitoring progress.

A challenge for all ERMs is to keep up with business developments and business evolution. As more and more businesses become data driven, with a large portion of digital operations, the speed of change has increased significantly. This development has made many organisations' ERMs incomplete or even obsolete. The same is also true regarding compliance risks in the ERM since many industries that formerly did not have to consider regulations must now conduct business according to data protection legislation, anti-bribery legislation, anti-money-laundering legislation and so on. Consequently, the ERM must be updated to show how compliance risk is related to classic business risks.

Every company in a competitive market will have a long list of risks stemming from a wide variety of areas. These could be risks regarding competition, currency fluctuations, natural catastrophes, fatal accidents and so on. From a business risk perspective, data protection risks did not previously come to the attention of the CEO or the board, because the business as such was not affected by disregarding the privacy or data protection of data subjects. That has changed dramatically with the GDPR.

For an organisation to evaluate both traditional risks and the newer data protection risks, all risks must be transferred to the same risk management system. In this respect, data protection risk management is still quite immature – and it throws out a lot of challenges.

DIFFERENT BUSINESS IMPACTS OF DATA PROTECTION RISKS AND COMPLIANCE RISKS

We have now looked at the different types of risk and how they relate to each other. In this section, we will briefly examine different forms of negative impact these risks can have if they materialise.

Fines and compensation (indemnification)

If you only know one thing about the GDPR, it is probably something about 'high fines'. But fines will in most cases be the last resort, especially if we are referring to the highest fines possible (i.e. 20 million euros or 4% of global annual turnover, whichever is higher). As is generally the case in systems of this kind, there is a staircase with a series of other corrective measures or sanctions that may apply before a company is hit with the maximum fine. It's a bit like driving too fast in your car. If you drive 1 kilometre per hour (km/h) too fast, you will probably just be told to lower your speed, but if you go 100 km/h while passing a school you will probably both get a very high fine and lose your driving licence for some months. Between these points, there's a scale with more and more severe consequences. It is the same with the GDPR. The more severe a breach is, the more severe the sanction will be.

Neglecting the rights of data subjects altogether and ignoring decisions by the authorities will be seen as severe breaches, while accidental small breaches without any severe consequences for data subjects will probably only render a correctional comment from the authorities. Based on the current case law, this is exactly how the authorities have used the various sanctions available to them.

Fines are not the only direct monetary consequence that can result from a personal data breach, and they may not even be the most expensive. In contrast to fines, compensation to data subjects has no maximum and entirely depends on the severity and number of affected data subjects. In some of the more notable breaches in previous years, breaches by British Airways, easyJet and Marriott Hotels led to millions of data subjects suffering negative effects by having their personal data stolen (including credit card information). Even minor compensation to each data subject can add up to a high amount in the end. It will also create a lot of administration to actually execute.

Reputation and trust

Besides different forms of direct sanctions the authorities can impose on an organisation, such as fines, non-compliance can also have consequences for a company's brand and commercial interests.

Take, for instance, the breach by Facebook and Cambridge Analytica, revealed in 2018. It had severe consequences for the involved companies. Cambridge Analytica had to close down its whole business and Facebook's CEO, Mark Zuckerberg, was interrogated by both the US Congress[3] and the European Parliament.[4] In the UK, Richard Allan, European policy chief of

---

3   'Mark Zuckerberg testimony: Senators question Facebook's commitment to privacy' (2018), *The New York Times*, 10 April, https://www.nytimes.com/2018/04/10/us/politics/mark-zuckerberg-testimony.html.

4   'Follow-up answers from Facebook after the meeting between EP leaders and Zuckerberg' (2018), European Parliament News, 24 May, https://www.europarl.europa.eu/news/en/press-room/20180524IPR04204/follow-up-answers-from-facebook-after-zuckerberg-s-meeting-with-leading-meps.

Facebook, was questioned by the UK Parliament. During the inquiries, he stated, 'I'm not going to disagree with you that we've damaged public trust with some of the actions we've taken.'[5] Such a statement from the top official spokesperson for Facebook in the EU makes this case a good example of the reputational risks of bad data protection practices.

That being said, examinations of the stock price of companies that have experienced bad publicity indicate that there is normally no long-term effect on interest in investing in such companies. This might sound strange, but examining the stock price just before and at different intervals after a breach reveals that in most cases the breach has no effect on the stock price at all in the mid to long term (see Figure 4.1).

Figure 4.1 Changes in stock price for five companies with known breaches

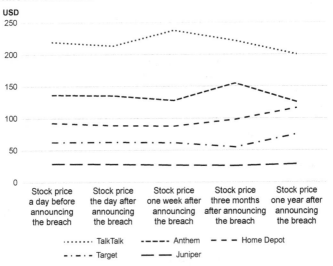

5   A. Hern (2018), 'Fake news inquiry: Facebook questioned by MPs from around the world – as it happened', *The Guardian*, 27 November, https://www.theguardian.com/technology/live/2018/nov/27/fake-news-inquiry-facebook-to-face-mps-from-around-the-world-mark-zuckerberg-live-updates?page=with:block-5bfd2f03e4b045afb4424ccc.

But does stock price tell the whole truth? According to a survey conducted by FireEye in May 2016, around three quarters (73%) of consumers said that they would likely stop purchasing from an organisation if they found out that a theft of their data had been caused by a lack of board-level attention to security. Negligent data handling and negligent data protection would also drive away three quarters (74%) of consumers.[6] A similar survey was conducted in 2014 by Deloitte. According to this survey, 59% of consumers stated that a single data breach would negatively affect their likelihood of buying from a consumer products company.[7] As public awareness of data protection issues is increasing in most parts of the world, these figures will likely go up even more.

What do these surveys tell us? Being a trusted custodian of personal data will be of increasing importance in the years to come and will probably stay at a high level as long as we have a digitised world. Abuses of trust will probably lead to organisations getting increasingly bad reputations as people are becoming more and more privacy aware. This will, in turn, lead to consequential losses, such as decreased sales.

In this regard, not only regulators but also data subjects will hold organisations accountable for data protection. Reputational damage may in turn affect organisations' relationships with business partners, employees, insurers, industry watchdogs, national governments, workers' unions and professional organisations.

Business continuity

Business continuity is of the essence for all companies, and disruptions should be avoided since they will decrease earning ability.

---

6   'Beyond the bottom line: The real cost of data breaches' (2016), FireEye, https://www.fireeye.com/current-threats/cost-of-a-data-breach/wp-real-cost-data-breaches.html, p. 11.

7   P. Conroy et al. (2014), *Building Consumer Trust: Protecting Personal Data in the Consumer Product Industry*, Deloitte, https://www2.deloitte.com/content/dam/insights/us/articles/consumer-data-privacy-strategies/DUP_970-Building-consumer-trust_MASTER.pdf, p. 5.

As good data quality is a prerequisite for all data-driven companies, data should always be kept up to date and with minimal errors. From the business continuity perspective, good data protection benefits from and goes hand in hand with good data quality. Therefore, there are multiple reasons why data governance should be good from the highest level down to individual data sets and data points.

From the GDPR perspective, there are two main threats that could entail disruption to the business. The first is the right of the supervisory authority to carry out investigations in the form of data protection audits. The audit right includes the ability to order the controller to provide any information the authority requires.

The second is the right of the supervisory authority to order a controller to make processing operations compliant with the GDPR. The decision can be coupled with a specified time frame and a temporary or definitive limitation or ban on processing.

For data-driven companies, avoiding a decision to ban a processing activity central to the business is likely to be a high priority. Such a decision could mean the business as a whole stops. Since a ban will probably only be considered if there are great risks to data subjects, it is likely to have an immediate effect after the decision is taken and as such the business may, during the enforcement action and dialogue with the supervisory authority, have time to amend the processing before it needs to stop, permanently or until the authority has assessed and approved the changed processing.

A decision by the authority to bring some specific data processing into compliance could be paired with a temporary ban until the nature of the processing has been changed. But, even if there is no such ban, the processing cannot continue since it is not compliant, so it must stop until it is updated. As changing the processing will probably take resources as well as time and money, this is a clear business disrupter.

Even an audit, regardless of whether it is a thorough audit done on the premises or a desktop audit (which is usually done remotely and only concerns high-level documents), will require extensive resources if an organisation is unprepared. How many resources it will require is related to how closely your organisation follows the accountability principle in the GDPR (see Chapter 1). If you have all the necessary documentation in order and your processing is conducted in line with this documentation, the audit will 'only' take the time required to gather the applicable or required information. But, if you don't have pre-prepared assessments and documentation, it will probably be quite an extensive task to answer the questions posed by the authority and thus the risk of business disruption will be higher.

SUMMARY

This chapter has covered the distinctions between different forms of risk and how to assess risk. A risk consists of an event and the likelihood and impact of that event.

From a data perspective point of view, it is the risks to data subjects that should be assessed. But, it is important to understand how these are linked to other types of risk – for example, business risks. It is ultimately the business that should make all decisions in relation to risks, whether data protection risks, compliance risks or business risks.

DPO's tips

- Some risks will be the same for different processing activities within an organisation. Creating a list of these risks will help you in the assessment of new processing activities. You can also combine this list with previously used mitigating actions. You will eventually have an extensive list of risks and suggestions for mitigating actions. Such lists will also help the business to choose suitable solutions early in the process.

- Make your highest level of management aware of what you understand the organisation's current data protection risk appetite to be – or point out the lack of a clear statement on risk appetite if appropriate. Ask them to update the organisation's data protection risk appetite (if required) and document it. Such documentation will help you in conducting risk assessments and reporting on data protection risks. The risk appetite might change over time and depend on the business area, so make sure you revisit the question at appropriate intervals.

5 REVIEWING YOUR ORGANISATION'S DATA PROTECTION PRACTICES

As we stated in Chapter 2 in the section 'Monitoring compliance', reviews are an indispensable tool for monitoring and verifying the proper implementation of data protection legislation. We have deliberately chosen not to use the term 'audits', in order not to mix this process up with internal audit functions or audits by a supervisory authority.

Generally, reviews (or audits) can be either internal (also called 'soft') or external. An external review is an assessment carried out by a national data protection authority[1] or by a third-party auditor.[2] In contrast, an internal review is conducted by the organisation itself.

The reviews you will lead and/or conduct as the data protection officer (DPO) are internal. In this chapter, we will only describe internal reviews, and you will learn how to plan and execute a data protection review. You will also learn how to formulate a review report and why such review reports are important. See the section 'Investigative powers' in Chapter 1 for more information on the supervisory authorities' investigative powers – for example, the power to conduct reviews and on-site visits.

Ultimately your reviews should examine your organisation's compliance with applicable data protection legislation, such

---

1 For further reading about authorities' audits, we recommend *A Guide to ICO Audits* (2018), Information Commissioner's Office, https://ico.org.uk/media/for-organisations/documents/2787/guide-to-data-protection-audits.pdf.

2 It is common practice for processors to have third-party audits and to contractually give their controllers the right to receive a copy of the audit report.

as the General Data Protection Regulation (GDPR). The reviews should focus on data protection practices, either on the governance level or the implementation level. In other words, your reviews should either focus on whether your policies and processes are compliant, or whether your organisation is following these policies and processes. The review report should show the current state and reveal gaps and risks that require action concerning legal requirements and internal requirements, as stipulated in the organisation's policies and instructions. As such, the value of the review report is diverse. For example, it can measure your data protection programme's effectiveness, demonstrate compliance with laws, reveal gaps in your data protection practice, and provide a base for improvement plans, risk mitigation and decision-making.

Some reviews should be conducted periodically, to ensure that you have a current, accurate understanding of your organisation's data flows, information-handling practices and data protection positioning. Other reviews may be required in response to an incident or a revelation of malpractice.

CONDUCTING AN INTERNAL DATA PROTECTION REVIEW

The process of conducting a review can be divided into six distinct phases: planning, preparation, execution, reporting, follow-up and what we call 'methodology assessment'. The six phases are part of a review cycle, as shown in Figure 5.1.

Before we examine the different phases, it is worth emphasising that a review should always reflect how the organisation's practice stands against legal requirements, internal policies or best practices – for example, widely accepted industry standards such as the Generally Accepted Privacy Principles (GAPP) (for more on GAPP see Chapter 6).

Figure 5.1 Internal review cycle (recurring reviews)

Review planning

The planning and preparation phases are the most important in a review. Good planning and preparation will not only facilitate efficiency but also increase the quality of the result of the review. Good planning will also ensure minimum business disruption.

The most basic part of the planning phase is the vital aspect of obtaining senior management buy-in. Their support will be critical to the success of the review.

During the planning phase, you should decide on the scope of the review. You could, for example, review the whole lifecycle of some specific category of personal data the organisation is processing and determine whether it is done appropriately at each step. Alternatively, you could examine all processing done by a specific department.

When you decide the scope of the review, it is important to remember that an incomplete or improperly conducted review creates false impressions of the current state and may lead to wrong decisions and prioritisation. Thus, don't bite off more than you can chew.

Once you have decided on a suitable scope for your data protection review, you should start looking at what resources will be necessary to conduct the review from preparation to reporting and follow-up. In conjunction, you should consider whether the review should be conducted using an internal team or external consultants, or a mix of both.[3] There are advantages to all three approaches and the choice will depend on the scope of the review as well as available resources in terms of people and budget. Before you decide, you should consider that a review is a quite time-consuming task and usually involves several different activities, including meeting and interviewing various stakeholders. As the outcome of the review will be inaccurate if different parts of the organisation are examined at different times, it is important to conduct the review in a time-efficient manner.

This could be one reason for hiring consultants to conduct an internal review rather than carrying out the review yourself. While you probably have a better knowledge of the structure and functioning of your organisation, consultants (e.g. from the Big Four[4]) maybe more experienced in carrying out these reviews and may be able to devote more time and resources to them. Moreover, external consultants are likely to approach the matter with a more open, independent and unbiased mindset. Hiring a consultant in the form of an experienced data protection auditor could be more expensive but on the other hand more efficient in terms of relevance, quality and time. In many situations, it may be advisable to have an experienced data protection reviewer as project manager and assign internal resources for that person to use.

---

3 In the context of this book, we call these three strategies 'internal audits' since they are initiated by the organisation itself.

4 A term commonly used for the global accounting firms of Deloitte, Ernst & Young, KPMG and PricewaterhouseCoopers.

Another important aspect to consider before you start your review is what the expected outcome for the organisation is. Do you 'just' want to measure data protection maturity (see Chapter 2) or is your aim rather to raise awareness and influence commitment at the top? Most often you will probably want to evaluate functions, processes, controls or services. In all cases, the outcome should include a list of recommendations and actions.[5] The scope and choice of method must be aligned with expectations.

During this phase, you should also decide whether you will only review your governing structure via a gap analysis (see Chapter 2) – sometimes referred to as a policy review – or whether you will examine the effectiveness of the pieces of the structure (e.g. whether your data protection training is having the desired effect).

Review preparation

When the planning is complete, it is time to prepare for the actual review. This could be seen as a continuation of the planning phase, but on a much more granular level. The better the preparation, the more efficient the review will be. Efficiency is of the essence here, since the review report will show a snapshot of the situation at the time of information gathering. Based on the decisions made during the planning phase, the preparation phase mainly consists of deciding how to gather information, and identifying and contacting relevant stakeholders.

Information gathering

There are multiple ways of gathering the necessary input for a review – for example, questionnaires or surveys, in-depth interviews, group discussions and workshops. An efficient way is often to invite stakeholders of a specific process to a workshop and follow the process through step

---

5 *Global Technology Audit Guide 5: Managing and Auditing Privacy Risks* (2006), Institute of Internal Auditors, https://www.iia.nl/SiteFiles/IIA_leden/Praktijkgidsen/GTAG5.pdf, p. 14.

by step to establish how information is being collected, used, disclosed and destroyed. The importance of having **all** relevant stakeholders in the room at the same time cannot be overestimated.

Another common way to collect information is via questionnaires. This can be a good choice if it is hard to get all stakeholders together in the same workshop. Remember to focus on objective questions or measures rather than subjective elements. You should also keep the number of questions to the minimum necessary. It is much better to get answers from all stakeholders to slightly fewer questions than to have only a few stakeholders respond to a lot of questions. You could also begin by sending a few screening questions and then follow up with more questions sent to a smaller group of stakeholders.

Both for workshops and for questionnaires, it is often useful to accompany your invitations with general instructions plus guidance on key terminology, the purposes and importance of the review, and the purpose of each review question or of the workshop. The instructions and questions should be kept simple – remember that the participants won't know half as much as you do about data protection.

Try not to use open questions but instead ask narrow questions. For example, instead of asking 'What personal data do you process?', it may be better to ask 'Do you collect names and other details from our customers?' Don't ask 'What is the legal basis for the processing?' but do ask 'Do we enter into a contract with customers?' Don't ask 'Are we transparent about our processing activities?' but do ask 'Do we give customers information about our collection of their information?' This is because while you may know the legal terminology and what specific words mean, there will most likely be misconceptions about data protection among the participants.

It is also worth mentioning the growing field of intelligent software (e.g. Aigine or BigID), which could help you to find more sophisticated ways of gathering information. Such software could help with such things as finding personal data in unstructured material or learning what tracking technologies your organisation uses.

Identifying stakeholders

Finding the right stakeholders for a review can be a challenging task in larger organisations. First of all, you must map all relevant business units and their functions. Once this is done, it is important to get a grip on how the data processing activities are structured within and/or across different units and departments. For example, one challenge may be that centralised databases or systems are shared among business units or even legal entities. In such cases, the system owner may not be aware of all use cases and you will have to identify all data owners that use the system. Your record of processing activities (ROPA) could help you to find the relevant business units and the relevant stakeholders.

Review execution

It is time to start the actual review. If you have not informed all stakeholders, now is the time to do so. The actual execution of the review will probably be the most time-consuming part of the review, as collecting information can be a daunting task – not least since considerable time and effort are required for respondents to provide comprehensive and meaningful responses.

Once you have gathered the necessary information, it is time to evaluate it. At this stage, you will find yourself with a pile of information, questionnaires, meeting notes and so on. All of this must be carefully reviewed to identify any gaps or contradictions in the responses. In some cases, further clarification or additional information will need to be sought. How the evaluation should be done will depend on the scope of the review. When you have drawn your conclusions, it is time to get them into a report.

Review reporting

Your reports should follow a fixed structure that readers can recognise from report to report. The exact structure will probably depend on your organisation's practices and templates. Nevertheless, your review report should include a description of each of the phases of the review cycle, beginning with the methodology and scope and moving on to the results of the review (the 'findings') – for example, gaps in compliance or good practices.

Before you start to write the report, you should ensure you are clear on the identity of your audience or the recipient(s) of the report. Even though the GDPR states that the DPO should report to the highest management level, it is not necessary for all reports to have the top management as their core audience. In many cases it may be the relevant involved stakeholders. As a review report will probably highlight shortcomings or non-compliance, it is wise to keep the recipient group as small as possible. You could even consider sending only parts of the full report to different stakeholders, according to who is affected by each part.

Before you finalise the report, you must send a draft to all stakeholders for comments and give them the chance to correct any inaccuracies. The review report must accurately reflect the business practices since you don't want to end up with objections based on factual errors.

After you have presented potential gaps, the review report should also include prioritised recommendations in the form of clear suggested actions on how to address the gaps, also referred to as 'mitigating actions'. These actions should, in turn, be used as feedback on business processes to improve performance regarding compliance. The report could also, on an aggregated level, refer to identified risk areas (e.g. vendors/processors or transfers to third countries). The report must be a basis for action, otherwise it is likely to end up just sitting on a shelf.

185

Once the final review report has been circulated to the relevant stakeholders, it may be a good idea to gather them together in a meeting to discuss the results and action plans.

Review follow-up

Depending on the outcome of the review and the action list, follow-up could be done either through self-assessments or through more formal reviews at future dates.

All follow-ups should be conducted on an action-by-action basis – that way, it can clearly be identified when an action has been completed and can be closed. It should be noted, however, that the person accountable for a gap may decide to accept it rather than take the recommended action. If that is the case, it should be documented accordingly and the action can be closed.

The follow-up phase lasts until all actions are closed.

Review methodology assessment

The last phase is all about the lessons learned during the review. What worked well and what didn't work? This could be anything from individual questions in a questionnaire to the layout of the review report. If possible, you should also conduct an assessment of the resources used, to establish whether they were effectively used or whether there could be ways of using them more efficiently.

This phase is mainly carried out for your own sake. However, given that reviews should be done with minimal business disruption, improving efficiency review by review will also have a positive impact on the business.

Checklist for conducting a review

- Draw up a review plan. Include:
  - the objective of the review (e.g. compliance with applicable laws and standards);
  - the scope of the review (e.g. certain legal entity, certain service/product or documentation);
  - the method and the data protection framework you have chosen (e.g. GAPP or the Privacy Maturity Model created by the American Institute of Certified Public Accountants (AICPA) and the Canadian Institute of Chartered Accountants (CICA)[6]);
  - the dates for an on-site review;
  - the high-level agenda;
  - details of preparations required (e.g. background information, interviewees and points of contact);
  - the plan for delivery.
- Hold a pre-review call with stakeholders to agree on the review plan.
- One week before the meetings, interviews or workshops, send the appropriate documentation and a detailed schedule.
- After the meetings, interviews or workshops, send a letter of thanks to all participants.
- Draft the report and send it to stakeholders for comments.
- Finalise the report and make sure you include recommendations.

---

6 *AICPA/CICA Privacy Maturity Model* (2011), American Institute of Certified Public Accountants and Canadian Institute of Chartered Accountants, https://iapp.org/media/pdf/resource_center/aicpa_cica_privacy_maturity_model_final-2011.pdf.

SUMMARY

In this chapter, we have discussed the essential aspects of preparing, executing and reporting reviews of your organisation's data protection practices. For example, we emphasised the importance of having a clear understanding of the business strategy and scope, identifying relevant stakeholders, ensuring the stakeholders acknowledge the facts of your findings, and verifying that your reports are clear and include suggestions for action. Most importantly, do not act in a vacuum, do your very best to support the stakeholders in your organisation and present actionable measures.

6 STANDARDS, FRAMEWORKS AND TOOLS

This chapter examines a selection of data protection standards and frameworks that may be useful to you as a data protection officer (DPO). It cannot be stressed enough that it is not a good idea to develop your compliance strategy and action plan by addressing the legal requirements and obligations one at a time. Rather, the best way is to adopt a holistic, business-centred perspective, supported by a standard or framework.

STANDARDS

ISO 27701

ISO 27701 ('Security techniques') is an extension for organisations that already hold ISO 27001 ('Information security management') certification. It is aimed at helping organisations to address the specific obligations and requirements relating to the processing of personal data. The standard is not built on the obligations and requirements in the General Data Protection Regulation (GDPR), and your organisation must make its own assessment of the extent to which adherence to the standard also results in compliance with the GDPR.

BS 10012:2017

The British Standards Institution (BSI) is the national standards body of the UK. BS 10012:2017 ('Personal information management system') provides a framework that improves compliance with data protection requirements and good practice – in particular, those of the GDPR. It should be emphasised that, as its title indicates, it is a standard for information governance and management. Each part of the system follows the 'plan, do, check, act' cycle, which aims to ensure continuous improvement.

FRAMEWORKS

A framework is in many respects similar to a standard but is more of a set of principles than actual requirements. The content and principles in a framework must be converted into actionable and measurable internal requirements. This section takes a look at a key framework that could help your organisation to structure its data protection operations and practice.

Generally Accepted Privacy Principles

The Generally Accepted Privacy Principles (GAPP) is a framework that any organisation can use to design and manage a privacy programme. GAPP was developed by the American Institute of Certified Public Accountants (AICPA) and the Canadian Institute of Chartered Accountants (CICA).[1] There are 10 principles, each supported by objective, measurable criteria. There are 73 criteria in total. Examples of controls are provided for each criterion.

GAPP combines internationally recognised privacy principles, referencing some significant privacy legislation with established data protection best practices. The framework is unique in how it sets data protection concepts within a business context, which makes it easy to use when planning, managing and evaluating an organisation's data protection compliance. This makes GAPP particularly valuable to

1 See 'Generally Accepted Privacy Principles' (2009), American Institute of Certified Public Accountants and Canadian Institute of Chartered Accountants, https://www.cpacanada.ca/-/media/site/operational/ms-member-services/docs/00250-generally-accepted-privacy-principles.pdf?la=en&hash=284D936484F7D77307F80A9951E015D551B62DBC.

international organisations that need to adhere to various local laws.

The GAPP principles are:

1. Management
2. Notice
3. Choice and Consent
4. Collection
5. Use, Retention and Disposal
6. Access
7. Disclosure to Third Parties
8. Security for Privacy
9. Quality
10. Monitoring and Enforcement

You could use the GAPP framework when establishing your long-term data protection programme, when evaluating a certain area of your organisation, or when evaluating and reporting on your organisation's compliance level. Figure 6.1 illustrates a six-step process for using GAPP with an additional optional step. These steps are:

1. **Determine your organisation's risk profile:** we recommend starting a GAPP exercise by assessing your organisation's risk profile and determining the appropriate risk maturity level that your organisation should have as a desired target for its compliance programme and for evaluation of the audit. A high risk profile is indicative of a strong requirement to achieve compliance with data protection obligations. Consider: What field of business is your organisation active in? Is it prone to a high level of third-party attacks, subject to exacting media scrutiny or regulated by strict legislative requirements? Does it require a high level of trust among the public and/or its customers? What is the organisation's risk tolerance? What ambition does the organisation have concerning its compliance programme?

2. **Inventory of data:** start with your record of processing activities (ROPA). What data do you hold and what obligations apply to this data? Prepare charts showing the flow of personal data, including points of storage, interfaces, outputs, access and so on. Each flowchart should also identify any assets and system components (such as networks, applications, databases and end-user interfaces).

3. **Risk assessment:** identify operational risks based on an analysis of the ROPA.

4. **Assess compliance against each GAPP criterion:** review your existing documentation, policies and information security controls relevant to the criteria in the GAPP framework. When auditing based on GAPP, the auditor can assess the adequacy of existing data protection controls and recommend whether any remedial action is needed.

5. **Strengthen the GAPP controls:** on the basis of the challenges identified and remedies needed, make recommendations to management and ensure that progress against these recommendations is regularly reviewed.

6. **Measure and monitor GAPP controls and remedial actions:** you cannot manage what you do not measure. The 10th GAPP principle relates to monitoring, and the AICPA and CICA provide numerous examples of how a range of data protection considerations can involve management.[2]

Figure 6.1 Six + one steps in using GAPP

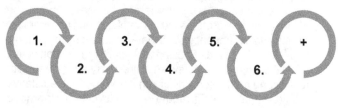

---

2   *Ibid.*, pp. 12–22.

+ **Optional step of attestation:** it is often considered good practice to provide stakeholders – such as investors and business partners – with either management's assertion of compliance or some details of the auditor's findings.

TOOLS

At some point in time, you will find it necessary to seek help, whether to keep up with legislative developments or to ensure appropriate governance of your data protection programme. This section briefly introduces some of the tools available to support you. See also the online resources in Appendix 3.

Privacy management software

Privacy and data protection tools are, broadly speaking, software and services that can assist DPOs in the execution of their work.[3] These can be divided into two categories: tools for the administration of the work and tools that help the DPO in the execution of actions. Most vendors have focused on the latter category, but our experience tells us it is probably the administrative part of the job where tools are most useful to the DPO.

For a comprehensive list of tool vendors, consult the annual Privacy Tech Vendor Report published by the International Association of Privacy Professionals (IAAP) (see https://iapp.org/resources/article/privacy-tech-vendor-report).

Administrative tools can also be called privacy programme management (PPM) solutions.[4] To qualify for this category, a tool must include some form of dashboard that helps to

---

3 We do not have any personal interest in any of these tools.

4 This is the name used by the IAPP.

operationalise the tasks of the DPO to make them more efficient.

OneTrust

OneTrust consists of a platform with multiple individual tools for almost any aspect of data protection management. These can be used individually or linked together.

TrustArc

TrustArc is built on three legs: a technology platform, a consulting service and certifications. The platform consists of several individual modules that can either be used individually or added on top of each other. It is possible to integrate with several other applications and hosting environments. TrustArc also offers a knowledge service based on its research.

BigID

BigID is software that uses machine learning to find, categorise and document personal data. It can help an organisation to create an inventory of its personal data and data flow maps.

Privacy1

Privacy1 is built on two main concepts. One is decentralised data mapping and a centralised access management process built on the data mapping. The other is administrative tools for various areas of data protection management – for example, data subject access requests (DSARs), privacy notices, a privacy dashboard, and a DPO task and control module.

LEGAL RESOURCES

Keeping up to date with legalities can be both time-consuming and difficult. There's only one easy way: let somebody else do it. There are numerous excellent online resources, such as blogs, online services and newsletters, that you can subscribe to. There are also enforcement trackers, which may be useful depending on your specific data protection interest.

Consult the online resources in Appendix 3 for more information.

SUMMARY

In this chapter, we have discussed how you can use established standards, frameworks and tools to manage a data protection programme in your organisation, or how to use parts of these and implement them in your organisation's data protection practices. We have also provided some tips on how to keep up to date with legal development in the field of data protection.

7   DATA PROTECTION OFFICER CASE STUDIES

In this chapter, we will put some of the legal theory into practice. In two different scenarios, both based on our experience from real cases, we will try to solve a few issues and situations that many data protection officers (DPOs) are confronted with. The suggestions we give might not be the most suitable in a similar situation in your organisation, partly because small details often have a great impact on how to solve cases, and partly due to differences in risk appetite between organisations. Regardless, we have tried to keep such possibilities to a minimum when choosing the case studies.

CASE STUDY 1: ALPHA LTD – INTERNATIONAL IT ORGANISATION

Alpha Ltd is an international group of companies that provides businesses and consumers with various web-based IT services and IT applications. Alpha has 1,200 employees overall and is headquartered in London, UK, with sales offices in 24 countries, mainly in the EU but also in Norway, China and the USA. The technical development is located in the UK and Hungary while back-office support is provided by a sub-contractor situated in Bengaluru, India.

Information security has long been a priority for the management, but the DPO role is new. Alpha has an in-house legal department at its London headquarters of five full-time lawyers and an information security department of nine full-time IT security professionals. Having found no internal candidate who could fulfil the requirements of the DPO role as set out by the General Data Protection Regulation (GDPR), the management has chosen to hire a new, experienced data protection professional as the DPO. Heidi has been evaluated, qualified and selected as Alpha's DPO based on the requirements we looked at in Chapter 2.

Alpha has advanced plans to outsource the operations of its internal IT environment to the US-based IT consulting firm Managed Services Inc, which will use the American cloud service provider YNSecure Inc as a sub-contractor. Alpha has recently acquired a Spanish company that uses biometric data as a passcode to validate the identification of employees when they gain access to its offices.

Alpha collects personal data through the use of web-based services where customers create user accounts. Alpha also collects data from third parties, such as the market research company InfoMiners, to enhance the profiles of its customers and enable it to create segments of customers based on derived social status, income level and estimated purchase power. Alpha uses this information to create campaigns and target advertising. Diagnostic data is generated through customers' use of Alpha's services and programs if customers have not objected to such processing. The processing is done in YNSecure's servers as close to the country of residence of the customer as possible, while support matters are processed in Bengaluru.

Alpha processes the personal data of candidates in its recruitment processes as well as the data of its employees, consultants and former employees. Alpha's security and operations centre (SOC) takes pride in the level of IT security implemented throughout the organisation. In particular, there is excitement about the promise of a new intelligent data loss prevention (DLP) solution that monitors employees' behaviours when they are using their company laptop, mobile and other devices.

Initial assessment of compliance level

After updating her knowledge of current industry trends, Heidi starts by interviewing the management and other key personnel, such as data owners and process owners. She wishes to understand the motivations and ambitions behind Alpha's data protection compliance and what objective the organisation has that the data protection programme should aim to support. She also learns how the governance of data protection compliance is organised and what resources are at her disposal. She finds that the head of the in-house legal department, Brian, and the chief information officer (CIO), Anna, are well situated in the organisation to provide her with valuable input. Heidi learns that while Alpha has well-put-together information security processes, its privacy perspective is lacking.

Among other things, there have been several incidents of phishing and social engineering attacks in which the intruders were likely to have gained access to employee account information and mailbox contents. The SOC's investigation is ongoing, and Heidi will be involved in the determination of any privacy implications of the IT attacks. The CIO, Anna, has some concerns about the proportionality of the DLP solution that has been implemented and advises Heidi to look into that project.

Using the techniques for putting together an action list in Chapter 2, Heidi proceeds to draft a list that will guide her work for the first few weeks in her new job. For this initial assessment, she does not take the time to compile evidence to support the findings and assumes that the policy, procedure and technology work more or less as intended. Evidence will be necessary when she performs a formal audit later in the year.

The first set of documents to review is the record of processing activities (ROPA), which paints an initial picture of how Alpha collects, uses and discards personal data and which technical assets that data resides on. Heidi meets with the data owners and system owners to review their records.

Where the information is incomplete or inconsistent, or where new information is revealed, Heidi requests that the data owners and system owners review the records to make them up to date and complete. (Note that this is an ongoing task that may take weeks, or even months, for the organisation to fully master. Often it is a parallel project that involves discovering how data is processed and updating the ROPA as the project proceeds. Be aware that this may be a task that your organisation would like to hand over to you to administer, but you should not accept it.)

When in a meeting with representatives of the SOC, Heidi initiates a data protection impact assessment (DPIA) to be performed by the system owner regarding the monitoring of employees' use of IT systems and assets. She makes a note to update the privacy information provided to Alpha's employees to ensure compliance with the GDPR's principle of transparency based on the result of the DPIA.

The externally facing data protection statement, or privacy notice, is another crucial document for Alpha, as it demonstrates its adherence to data protection legislation. With Alpha's collection of statistical data from the market research company InfoMiners in mind, Heidi adds a thorough review of the privacy notice and a review of Alpha's data processing agreement to her expanding action list.

Drawing from her knowledge of the GDPR's requirements and obligations (as set out in Chapter 1), Heidi reviews Alpha's operation in light of the fundamental data protection principles. Her starting point is again the ROPA. Applying a risk-based approach and focusing on the processing with the highest assumed privacy risks, she assesses each instance of processing – as described in the relevant records – by asking the following questions (based on the GDPR's principles):

- Is the processing lawful, fair and transparent?

- Is the processing for a specified, explicit and legitimate purpose?

- Is the personal data processed minimised to only include data that is adequate, relevant and necessary for the specified purpose?

- Is the personal data accurate and up to date?

- Is the personal data kept no longer than necessary?

- Is security appropriate to prevent unauthorised access to data, unwanted change of data and loss of data?

- Can the controller demonstrate compliance with principles 1–6?

Additionally, Heidi reviews the documentation against the principles behind data subjects' rights (see Chapter 3). When evaluating the public privacy notice, she adds to her action list to develop the text and include a section on data subjects' rights. The notice needs to clearly state Alpha's process for handling any requests made and its process for how to identify an individual who exercises their rights.

Before completing her initial compliance assessment, Heidi also considers implications of the ePrivacy Directive for marketing communication and reviews relevant employment and IT security legislation, standards and certifications.

Technical assessment

Alpha's outsourcing of its internal IT environment to an external partner is progressing well and Heidi is invited to a status meeting, where the transformation and transition (TNT) team presents the project's status and next steps. Alpha is about to close the negotiation of the purchase of network assets from a telecom operator. It intends to purchase network assets from the telecom operator as a service. The team is not, however, convinced of the benefits of purchasing additional security information and event management (SIEM) software, which would be provided directly by the hardware manufacturer SecurityBiz Inc. The SIEM software will provide real-time analysis of security alerts generated by applications and network hardware. This software will be installed in

Alpha's network assets and managed by the new outsourcing partner, Managed Services Inc.

When the project manager opens the agenda item on data protection, the room turns its attention to Heidi. Having listened carefully to the previous speakers and drawing from her experience of large-scale outsourcing, Heidi shares her concerns regarding the purchase.

It is fundamental to good IT security practices to have the capacity to identify and prevent unauthorised access attempts. Along the same line of reasoning, the GDPR obliges controllers to implement the appropriate security measures and technology to prevent unauthorised access to data, unwanted changes of data and loss of data. A SIEM solution such as the one at hand would be an excellent tool to mitigate that risk and Heidi is positive about acquiring the licences. From a privacy perspective, it will be important when configuring the software to find the right balance between collecting enough data to identify and prevent misuse of the IT system and adhering to the principle of data minimisation.

From the discussion in the room, it appears that it is not sufficiently clear how to regulate the data protection responsibility concerning the telecom operator and SecurityBiz Inc. The negotiator believes that the telecom operator is the counterparty in data protection matters; however, during a quick call to confirm this, representatives of the telecom operator refute such an interpretation. The meeting continues, and Heidi's advice is to ask SecurityBiz Inc to directly confirm what information that could be considered personal data is processed by the SIEM software. It is likely that at least unique identifiers such as MAC addresses and internal IP addresses are collected and monitored to allow authorised accounts and devices to gain access to the company network.

Furthermore, Heidi says that SecurityBiz may not be a processor as SecurityBiz only sells licences that will be installed on the premises. The TNT project should consider performing a DPIA on Managed Services' processing of data required to manage the SIEM software to strike the appropriate balance between protection and privacy in the configuration of the software. It should also examine to what extent Managed Services could use anonymised data. Lastly, the data processing agreement with Managed Services should be updated to reflect the new service of managing the SIEM software with the appropriate instructions and safeguards.

The meeting ends well, and Heidi is seen as a pragmatic, technology-savvy addition to Alpha's team.

DPO's tips

- Remember to base your advice on a holistic understanding of a situation. Too often, novice DPOs tend to provide advice that is too simplistic, not having completely understood the various elements of the data, protection and integrity that underpin the scenario.

- It is very important to document the facts, the analysis process and how a recommendation was reached. That way, if the recommendation turns out to be wrong, it is possible to work out what needs to change and the DPO can defend their decision-making process.

CASE STUDY 2: BETA AB – START-UP WITHIN THE E-HEALTH SECTOR

Peter is a trained engineer with more than 15 years' experience in senior positions in information security, IT development and compliance. He is the new DPO at Beta AB, a small enterprise in the e-health sector that supplies its solution to private and public healthcare companies in Sweden.

The company provides a smart meter, which is an application that monitors insulin levels with a web-based portal for healthcare professionals. The product is sold through the public health sector and is used by healthcare professionals and end-users, making self-care more secure and easy. The head office is in Stockholm and the technical development team is divided between this office and another in Latvia. Beta has 42 employees with the majority situated in Sweden. The product is cloud based and stores all of its data in a data centre in Frankfurt, Germany.

Technological development is at the heart of this company as the founder herself is an engineer. There is also a part-time resource dedicated to compliance concerning medical devices and healthcare. Beta has no in-house legal counsel, IT security competence or data protection capabilities. Having outsourced the role of DPO to an external consultant, Peter, Beta is confident that it is managing its resources efficiently. The long-term goal is to train the compliance resource to become a DPO over time, with the capable assistance of Peter.

The next major product upgrade will include the ability to predict end-users' health, forewarning them of a spike or dip in their insulin levels. Beta will be able to predict the occurrence of such incidents by tracking end-users' behaviours online and their browser patterns.

Beta collects personal data from end-users through the app and a medical device that measures insulin levels in the blood. It also collects personal data from the end-users' healthcare professionals through the web portal, in which they enter data obtained from the end-user in therapy. The end-user can rate their mood in the app during the day.

Initial assessment of compliance level

Start-ups are typically very strict with allocating resources, which is the case for Beta. Although Peter has received an appropriate mandate from the board of directors, there are limits to the resources at his disposal. Peter holds meetings with senior management to receive an up-to-date picture of the risks and any major concerns of the business. Hedda, the CEO, mentions that the basic level of security is there, but she feels that Peter should focus on managing Beta's potential risk exposure with regard to its major business customers as they have sensitive personal data. There are issues with improving the transparency of the processing of employees' personal data, but that should be of lower priority according to Hedda. Beta has not received any complaints or concerns from employees, and management calculates that the consequences of any breach should not be too severe. Adam, the CIO, has a similar opinion and states that the main service offering should be good enough and needs no major changes from a management perspective.

Peter has been in this situation many times before: an organisation with good intentions and limited resources. What the management and the board need from Peter as a DPO is his recommendations on how they should prioritise their resources. Peter's initial assessment is likely to find many areas for improvement, but he can focus the available resources on areas where they would best be invested. Peter needs to start by wrapping his head around the organisation, its risk profile and its resources so he can make recommendations on some tough prioritisations.

Making tough choices

These questions and suggestions may guide you to set priorities in view of the available time and resources – without compromising on the objectives of your organisation.

- What are the main trends in the current industry?

- What is the main strategic objective of the organisation? And how does data protection fit in and support that objective?

- Where would the impact of a violation of the data protection principles be most severe? Think about the privacy threats and privacy harms covered in Chapter 3 in the section on DPIAs.

- What use of data is the most valuable to the organisation?
- Could synergies be found by engaging in joint efforts with other divisions (e.g. procurement, IT, sales or legal)?
- To what extent can templates for standard situations and processes be used?
- Make short-term and long-term plans, and get management's buy-in.
- Whenever possible, review the priorities and expand the list to cover all relevant areas of the organisation.

Peter writes a report to present his initial assessment of Beta's compliance level. In line with the management's view, the security practices are good and the product fares fairly well in his assessment. As might be expected, Beta has poor documentation and is heavily dependent on the CIO to know how to manage a data breach, a change process and so on. This was expected and Peter partly puts this down to the organisation having a low maturity level, which his upcoming data protection programme will address.

He advises the management to focus on the service offering and to perform a DPIA for the planned upgrade. Also, he schedules training sessions for the company project managers so they can learn how to set up the ROPA. The CIO will receive coaching from Peter on how to set up an end-to-end DPIA process. The existing IT incident reporting process can be elevated into a personal data breach reporting process.

His creative mind and long experience help Peter to develop a good rapport with management. The CEO soon starts to think of her DPO as a team player and is keen on involving Peter in the early stages of the company's development of services and processes.

Technical assessment

Prior to the major upgrade to Beta's service offering, a DPIA is needed to ensure that the appropriate requirements are put in place. Peter arranges a four-hour workshop with the product team. The product owner has initiated the DPIA and has sent out materials for Peter to review before the meeting. The aim of the meeting is to go through the DPIA at a high level and allow for a more detailed discussion of the technical and organisational controls.

Beta has implemented a version of the DPIA process that is close to the approach championed by the French supervisory authority, the Commission Nationale de l'Informatique et des Libertés (CNIL). In this model, the risk assessment is performed by the product team with the opinion of the DPO and final validation by the CEO. The CNIL has published a series of handbooks on both technical assessments and good practices for implementing privacy impact assessment processes across an organisation.[1]

Peter is reassured by the structure and comprehensiveness of the DPIA report. He writes an initial assessment of the organisation's compliance based on the DPIA, looking at the following topics:

- Does the DPIA fulfil the criteria of the Article 29 Working Party (WP29) for an acceptable DPIA?[2]

- Can the DPIA be understood by the information and appendices referenced in the report?

- Do the risk assessments that have been conducted consider both data protection and privacy?

---

[1] *Privacy Impact Assessment (PIA): Knowledge Bases* (2018), Commission Nationale de l'Informatique et des Libertés, https://www.cnil.fr/sites/default/files/atoms/files/cnil-pia-3-en-knowledgebases.pdf.

[2] Article 29 Working Party (2017), *Guidelines on Data Protection Impact Assessment (DPIA) and Determining whether Processing is 'Likely to Result in a High Risk' for the Purposes of Regulation 2016/679*, Directorate C of the European Commission, https://ec.europa.eu/newsroom/article29/item-detail.cfm?item_id=611236, p. 22.

- Is there any feedback, internally or from customers, to be taken into consideration?
- Is the field of use of the DPIA considered a hot topic by the public and/or the authorities?

Going into the details, an analysis of the legal bases needs to be conducted. In the past, Beta has relied upon the performance of a contract as the main basis. Going forward, to implement the predictive behaviour function, both consent and legitimate interest will be required. Peter has prepared notes on a more extensive balance test for the legitimate interests assessment and he is eager to share them with the group.

Coming into the DPO role from an engineering background, Peter finds particular joy in technical assessments. He studied the technical control sections of the back-up service yesterday and made some observations on which he is keen to have the product owner's perspective. He believes that the logs do not contain the detail required under the GDPR and that they need to be enhanced. To prove traceability, Beta should set up a logging system for the application that retains records of data modifications and access by users and when they took place. Also, Beta should prohibit generic and shared identifiers, use strong passwords and give precedence to strong, two-factor authentication. Peter makes a note to review and potentially update the internal data protection policy for acceptable use of IT equipment, to appropriately inform Beta's employees about the traceability of logs.

Peter has studied the sections in the DPIA on encrypting databases and logical access control. The product team has explained the controls that are in place in the product via an Excel sheet, which lists all the technical and organisational controls available to Beta and the status of their implementation. Peter focuses on the controls applicable to the standard service offering. Overall, Beta has a good level of IT security but does not have sufficient access management controls. After reviewing the controls matrix, Peter believes that an investment in privileged access management would resolve the remaining data protection issues.

The product manager opens the meeting with a brief introduction to the product, its use of data, the identified weak spots and suggestions for mitigating action. For the most part, Peter concurs with what is said. He shares his concerns and provides practical advice on alternative technical solutions that are more privacy friendly. Peter is asked to provide a summary of his thoughts to share with the product owner that will facilitate the completion of the DPIA. The product owner will then evaluate the planned enhancement of the product with the DPO's notes in mind. Peter will then be asked to provide his formal advice on the risks as Beta's DPO and to suggest additional safeguards.

Data transfer and negotiating the data processing agreement

Peter receives an email with news about the data processing agreement from the external legal counsel he has enlisted. The agreement concerns Beta's most important customer, the public health authority in central Sweden. The authority is interested in a long-term collaboration with Beta. The business discussions have so far been fruitful and Beta's CEO has concluded a good-faith agreement with the customer. Peter is brought in to oversee the discussions on data, security and privacy and to ensure any discussions remain relevant to the product. Peter has put together a draft agreement taking into consideration the requirements under Article 28 of the GDPR and providing examples of clear instructions that specify Beta's use of personal data as a processor.

The external counsel makes certain recommendations on Peter's first draft. Peter recognises that it contains some good points and he incorporates the advice into the data processing agreement now being negotiated.

Peter is particularly pleased with the forum that has been created between the customer and Beta's customer team, who will work in close collaboration. Upon his suggestion, this forum will proactively plan for and resolve data protection issues. From experience, Peter has seen how efficient it is to have a team in place to plan any changes that occur in each long-term IT development project.

APPENDIX 1
OVERVIEW OF DATA PROTECTION CONCEPTS AROUND THE WORLD

Regardless of whether you are working in an organisation with mainly domestic business, or in a more international environment, you will need to know some basic facts about data protection around the world, not least to be able to do correct risk assessments.

The introduction of the GDPR affected not only the EU and Europe but also the rest of the world. All over the world, country after country is either updating its legislation or adopting new legislation, much more in line with the GDPR than before.

The following sections will give you a brief overview of how data protection looks around the world.

OVERVIEW

The international legal framework of privacy and data protection took form in 1948 with the Universal Declaration of Human Rights. Through this declaration, the international community first defined relevant and binding privacy norms, although at that time the norms did not include privacy of data. Since then, international organisations have helped to shape international data protection law. Leading international entities involved in this process have included the Organisation for Economic Co-operation and Development (OECD), the Council of Europe, the European Court of Human Rights (ECHR), numerous entities of the EU, and the Asia–Pacific Economic

Cooperation (APEC). Still, data protection legislation varies in important ways around the world.

Before we proceed to look at the situation around the world, it is relevant to note that the phrases 'information privacy law' and 'data privacy law' are the preferred terminology regarding data protection in the USA and many other countries outside the EU, whereas 'data protection law' is the favoured terminology in the EU.

NORTH AMERICA

The three largest countries in North America have taken three very different approaches to data protection. Not surprisingly, the USA has the least protection, but it is more surprising to observe that Mexico has a style of data protection legislation very similar to that of the EU. Somewhere in the middle, we find Canada.

The USA

Due to the lack of a comprehensive federal law on the collection and use of personal data, the USA has a wide range of federal and state laws and regulations. There are also several self-regulatory guidelines put in place by governmental agencies and industry groups, also known as 'best practices'. This patchwork of legislation is also diverse regarding its subjects – for example, some laws and regulations apply to consumer protection, whereas others apply to specific activities such as telemarketing and commercial emails.

Some notable acts are the Federal Trade Commission Act 1914 (which prohibits unfair and deceptive practices in the field of online privacy), the Electronic Communications Privacy Act of 1986 and the Computer Fraud and Abuse Act 1986.

In the aftermath of the Facebook and Cambridge Analytica case (see Chapter 4), there has been a rise in the number of requests for more federal regulation in the area of privacy.[1] Some of the specific areas under discussion are social media platforms, tracking technologies, artificial intelligence and self-driving cars.

Most recently we have also seen individual states drafting their own EU-style data protection laws. Most notable is the California Consumer Privacy Act 2018,[2] which replicates many of the rights and obligations in the GDPR.

Canada

In Canada, the fundamental protection of privacy is guaranteed by Sections 7 and 8 of the Canadian Charter of Rights and Freedoms 1982. Further specifics of data protection are laid down in the Privacy Act 1985, which regulates federal government institutions' collection, use and disclosure of personal information. This act also introduced a privacy commissioner with responsibility for investigating complaints and making recommendations within the scope of the act. The private sector is regulated by the Personal Information Protection and Electronic Documents Act 2000. This act is heavily inspired by the OECD Privacy Guidelines[3] as well as the 10 privacy principles stated in the Canadian Standards Association Model Code for the Protection of Personal Information. The principles are as follows:

1. Accountability
2. Identifying Purposes

---

1   T. Romm (2018), 'Lawmakers hope to use Facebook's "oil spill" privacy mishap to usher in sweeping new laws', *The Washington Post*, 23 March, https://www.washingtonpost.com/news/the-switch/wp/2018/03/23/lawmakers-hope-to-use-facebooks-oil-spill-privacy-mishap-to-usher-in-sweeping-new-laws/?noredirect=on&utm_term=.25559fc514ab; J. Rich (2018), 'Beyond Facebook: It's high time for stronger privacy laws', *Wired*, 8 April, https://www.wired.com/story/beyond-facebook-its-high-time-for-stronger-privacy-laws.

2   More information can be found at https://www.caprivacy.org.

3   'OECD Guidelines on the Protection of Privacy and Transborder Flows of Personal Data' (1980), Organisation for Economic Co-operation and Development, www.oecd.org/sti/ieconomy/oecdguidelinesontheprotectionofprivacyand transborderflowsofpersonaldata.htm.

3. Consent

4. Limiting Collection

5. Limiting Use, Disclosure, and Retention

6. Accuracy

7. Safeguards

8. Openness

9. Individual Access

10. Challenging Compliance[4]

Another act of importance is Canada's Anti-Spam Law 2010. Apart from prohibiting spam, the act prohibits data from being altered in transmission, as well as spyware, malware and botnets. It also includes penalties for the use of false or misleading representations in an email when promoting products and services.

Mexico

Article 16 of the Mexican Constitution proclaims the right of privacy to one's person, family, home, documents, possessions and communications. Moreover, the Federal Law on the Protection of Personal Data Held by Private Parties 2010 is an act based on the EU model, although it also includes the concept of 'habeas data'.[5] This, in short, is an individual right of a person whose data is processed to file a complaint with the courts to get their data rectified or deleted. The National Institute for Access to Information and Protection of Personal Data (INAI) is the supervisory body and has the right to issue decisions to protect the rights listed in the act. Similar regulation of the public sector was adopted in January

---

4 'PIPEDA fair information principles' (2019), Office of the Privacy Commissioner of Canada, https://www.priv.gc.ca/en/privacy-topics/privacy-laws-in-canada/the-personal-information-protection-and-electronic-documents-act-pipeda/p_principle.

5 'Data protection' (2014), Secretariat for Legal Affairs, Organization of American States, www.oas.org/dil/data_protection_privacy_habeas_data.htm.

2017 via the General Law of Protection of Personal Data in Possession of Obliged Subjects.

Other countries

In addition to the USA, Canada and Mexico, North America consists of 20 more countries and nine dependent territories. Some of them have enacted data protection laws, but most have not. Among those that have enacted laws are Costa Rica in 2011, the Dominican Republic in 2013 and Jamaica in 2017. But, as in the rest of the world, there is a growing trend towards adopting data protection laws in this region.

AUSTRALIA AND NEW ZEALAND

Although the Australian Constitution does not contain a provision on data protection, the Privacy Act 1988, amended in 2014, establishes the 13 Australian Privacy Principles, which are applicable to both the public and the private sectors. The principles set requirements for data quality, data security and how data may be used – for example, one principle deals with direct marketing.

The New Zealand Privacy Act 2020 similarly lays out a number of principles in its general framework for protecting individuals' privacy. These principles are very similar to those of Article 5 of the GDPR. New Zealand is considered to have adequate data protection by the European Commission by an adequacy decision (see Chapter 3).

FIVE EYES INTELLIGENCE ALLIANCE

The Five Eyes intelligence alliance consists of Australia, Canada, New Zealand, the UK and the USA. Its members share their national security intelligence. They also have particularly close collaboration and, to a certain extent, harmonisation in their national surveillance legislation. The alliance members have recently come under close scrutiny from the Court of

Justice of the European Union in the *Schrems II* and *Privacy International* rulings (see Chapter 3 for further details). In these cases, the court questioned the possibility of using the European Commission's Standard Contractual Clauses to make data available to suppliers outside the EU or the European Economic Area.

ASIA

Asia is very varied when it comes to data protection. Aside from examples of international co-operation such as the APEC Privacy Framework, individual countries on the Asian continent have developed their own regulations in the field of data protection. These national legislations are very different, from China at one end of the spectrum to Japan and South Korea at the other. It could be questioned how much data protection anyone in China has regardless of the legislation mentioned below. In contrast, South Korea will most likely be the next country to be considered to have adequate data protection by the European Commission. There is also a large number of countries with no legislation at all.

The following sections look at four examples of countries with legislation.

China and Hong Kong

China adopted its Cybersecurity Law in June 2017. The legislation aims to protect personal information, thus prompting organisations to focus not only on data security but also on individual data protection. The law additionally regulates the collection and use of personal data.[6] Also, China's Several Provisions on Regulating the Order of the Internet Information Service Market 2011 restricts entities that provide 'internet information services' from disclosing personal information

---

6 *Overview of China's Cybersecurity Law* (2017), IT Advisory KPMG China, https://assets.kpmg.com/content/dam/kpmg/cn/pdf/en/2017/02/overview-of-cybersecurity-law.pdf.

to third parties without prior consent. The regulations also limit the collection of data to what is strictly necessary and require entities to provide notice to users, establish security safeguards and inform the telecommunications authority in the case of data disclosures of a harmful nature.[7] However, the government collects a huge amount of personal data about Chinese citizens in order to calculate personal social scores.[8]

On 21 October 2020, China's National People's Congress published a consultation draft of the Personal Information Protection Law (known as the 'draft PIPL'). It draws extensively from the GDPR, introducing GDPR-like data subject rights, legal bases for processing, administrative sanctions, a DPO role and extraterritorial scope. If the law is enacted, it will be China's first comprehensive personal data protection law.[9]

Hong Kong, in contrast, has more vigorous protection of personal data. The Personal Data Ordinance 1997 regulates both the public and the private sectors of the territory and established the Office of the Privacy Commissioner for Personal Data. In 2012 the ordinance was amended in relation to notification and consent to the use, sale or transfer of data for direct marketing purposes, as well as significant penalties.[10]

---

7   'Several Provisions on Regulating the Market Order of Internet Information Services' (2011), Ministry of Industry and Information Technology, http://en.pkulaw.cn/display.aspx?cgid=164816&lib=law.

8   A. Ma (2018), 'China has started ranking citizens with a creepy "social credit" system – here's what you can do wrong, and the embarrassing, demeaning ways they can punish you', *Business Insider*, https://nordic.businessinsider.com/china-social-credit-system-punishments-and-rewards-explained-2018-4?r=US&IR=T.

9   See Gil Zhang and Kate Yin (2020), 'A look at China's draft of Personal Data Protection Law', IAPP, 26 October, https://iapp.org/news/a/a-look-at-chinas-draft-of-personal-data-protection-law; Todd Liao (2020), 'China's Personal Information Protection Law: Legislative update', Morgan Lewis, 27 October, https://www.morganlewis.com/pubs/2020/10/chinas-personal-information-protection-law-legislative-update.

10 See https://www.pcpd.org.hk.

Singapore

Singapore's Personal Data Protection Act 2012 was inspired by the EU's Data Protection Directive. The influence is noticeable in the act's structure and provisions, which are nearly identical to those of the directive. For example, the designation of a data protection officer is mandatory for all organisations subject to the act. Two crucial differences must be stated, however. In Singapore's act, there is no definition of sensitive data and the majority of the provisions do not apply to business information. Furthermore, there is no requirement for organisations to register the use of personal information with the authorities.[11]

Japan

In Japan, the right to privacy has been protected by the Constitution of Japan since 1963 and an Act on the Protection of Personal Information was adopted in 2005. This data protection law obliges companies to provide information about the use, storage and processing of personal data. Furthermore, all disclosures of data to third parties are subject to the fulfilment of legal requirements. The law was updated in 2017 – for example, with restrictions on the transfer of data to foreign countries and with a new requirement for prior consent for the collection of sensitive personal information.[12] Japan received its adequacy decision on 23 January 2019.

South Korea

As of late 2020, South Korea is the latest country being considered for an adequacy decision by the European Commission.

---

11 See Daniel J. Solove and Paul M. Schwartz (2017), *Privacy Law Fundamentals 2017*, Portsmouth, NH: IAPP, p. 282.

12 *Ibid.*, p. 280.

AFRICA AND THE MIDDLE EAST

Data protection has until very recently been very poor in Africa and the Middle East. However, in the aftermath of the introduction of the GDPR, quite a few African countries have started to draft or even adopt data protection legislation. As of late 2020, 27 countries on the continent had data protection legislation.[13]

Israel adopted its Protection of Privacy Act in 1981 and the Israeli Law, Information and Technology Authority (the Privacy Protection Authority) has existed since 8 May 2018.[14] The law demands certain databases to be registered with the government. The influence of the EU Data Protection Directive is prominent in the nation and led to Israel receiving an adequacy decision from the European Commission in January 2011.

Dubai enacted its data protection law in 2004 and amended it three years later by creating an Independent Office of the Commissioner of Data Protection and strengthening the act significantly.

SOUTH AMERICA

Just as in Mexico, many countries in South America have introduced the concept of 'habeas data'. It was first introduced in Brazil in the late 1980s and subsequently spread more widely. An example is Article 43 of the Constitution of the Argentine Nation, which proclaims the right to habeas data. As explained above, the core of the concept is the right of an individual to find out what information has been collected

---

13 'Data protection and privacy legislation worldwide' (2020), United Nations Conference on Trade and Development, https://unctad.org/page/data-protection-and-privacy-legislation-worldwide.

14 'About' (n.d.), Privacy Protection Authority, https://www.gov.il/en/Departments/about/about_ppa.

about them and to have data rectified or even erased under some circumstances.

Argentina also adopted the Law for the Protection of Personal Data in 2000. This is partly based on the EU Data Protection Directive and it made Argentina the first country in the continent to adopt a comprehensive data protection law.[15]

Brazil did not adopt any data protection legislation for some time, but it finally introduced a General Data Privacy Law in August 2018. This law is heavily influenced by the GDPR. Brazil is likely aspiring to be deemed to have adequate data protection by the European Commission.

DPO's tips

- If you want a shortcut to global knowledge on data protection legislation, a good starting point for a large number of countries is DLA Piper's web application Data Protection Laws of the World (see https://www.dlapiperdataprotection.com).

- As we have seen in this appendix, the level and maturity of data protection legislation are very diverse. Such diversity can be a challenge if a group of companies is about to roll out services to all entities in the group, in many different countries. In such cases, it will probably be difficult to introduce the service in every country; a better solution

15 *EX-2017-01309839-APN-DNPDP#MJ – Mensaje ley de protección de datos personales* [*Data Protection Law Message to Staff*] (2018), Argentine Republic National Executive Power, 19 September, https://www.argentina.gob.ar/sites/default/files/mensaje_ndeg_147-2018_datos_personales.pdf.

may be to assess the service in relation to a few countries with strict laws and apply the highest standard in each area to the whole group. With this approach, some very specific requirements may be missed in some countries, but on the whole you will be compliant and will have decreased your general risk level significantly, without having assessed all countries or adopted country-specific implementations.

APPENDIX 2
A REALISTIC DEVELOPMENT STAIRCASE

Here, we will describe an easy way for you to plan your development progress over six months or perhaps up to 18 or 24 months. The methodology is based on our own experience and influenced by various development schemes.

The main objective is to first set realistic goals and sub-targets and plan the execution of these to achieve the objectives. We call this the 'realistic development staircase'. The staircase consists of small, concrete steps that, one by one, will lead you to the new level or position to which you aspire.

Each step and the final goal should adhere to the principles of SMART – that is, specific, measurable, achievable, relevant and time-bound (see Chapter 2 for more on SMART). In our case the five principles can be explained as follows:

- **Specific:** each step in the realistic staircase must be specific in terms of what you should do to fulfil it. Each step should be a concrete action, not a mere aspirational goal. The more specific the better. You might start with a broader action and break it down into more specific sub-actions.

- **Measurable:** in our case, 'measurable' will most likely just mean 'done' or 'not done'. But, that said, it also means you should not have a step called, for example, 'Learn more about data protection.' Instead, it could be called 'Take the training on data protection at University X.'

- **Achievable:** this principle will help you to assess and exclude steps that are not realistic for you. Each step must be achievable based on the prior step and your previous experience and knowledge.

- **Relevant:** a step will only be relevant if it helps you to reach either the next step or the final goal. Examining each step from a relevancy perspective will help you to focus on the core steps and exclude things that it would be nice to have but that will not help you to reach your goal.

- **Time-bound:** as the whole idea behind the realistic development staircase is to set goals for your future development and tick them off step by step, each individual step and your end goal must have a timescale specified.

Let's have a look at how the realistic development staircase could be outlined for a newly appointed DPO (see Table A.1).

First of all, think of a long-term goal – approximately 18 months away. It could be that, even though you like your current position, you would in 18–24 months like to be in an even more challenging position or to have developed your current assignment within your organisation. Start to list your sub-targets and final goal, remembering that each of them must follow the SMART methodology. Start by writing down everything you can think of that would move your career in the right direction – things like updating your LinkedIn profile, achieving certifications, attending training, attending conferences, getting involved with privacy organisations, publishing articles and so on. Then, you can draw a staircase and write the first stage of your development plan (i.e. the lowest step), making sure it is as SMART as possible.

It can be very useful to adopt a granular view of the actions that are connected to each sub-target and your final goal. A good suggestion, therefore, is to create a three-column table with your sub-targets in one column, their deadlines in the next column and finally the more concrete actions you need to take to reach each sub-target in the third column.

Table A.1 Example of a realistic development staircase based on a start date of 1 November 2021

Target	Date	Concrete action
Become a member of the International Association of Privacy Professionals (IAPP)	31 December 2021	Go to iapp.com and register.
Update LinkedIn profile	31 January 2022	Go to linkedin.com and make sure all levels of your education and all former job positions are listed. Update your profile description.
Attend an IAPP KnowledgeNet Meeting	28 February 2022	Sign up for a KnowledgeNet Meeting either in your area or virtually.
Get certification with the IAPP: CIPP/E (European qualification) or CIPP/T (technical qualification)	31 July 2022	Buy the training book, sign up for a classroom course, sign up for the exam, and attend and pass the exam.

(Continued)

Table A.1 (Continued)

Target	Date	Concrete action
Write an article	31 October 2022	Research journals or blogs that publish similar articles to the one you would like to write. Contact three of these publications and ask whether they would be interested in an article on a specific topic. Write an article and send it to the journal or blog. Keep trying until you are accepted.
Speak at a conference	31 December 2022	Search for suitable conferences. Send in a proposal for a session. Speak at a session.
New position	3 September 2023	Look at job ads and speak to your contacts in the privacy community to find out about open positions. Apply for the most interesting positions. Get a job.

We have in this appendix given you some hands-on examples of how you can take your next step in your career, either within your organisation or on a different career path. We have also shared an example of how you can make a plan – and then execute that plan – to reach the next level in your career. Simply put, you should first think about where you would like to be in 12–24 months and then plan realistic steps to reach your goal.

APPENDIX 3
RESOURCES

KEY LEGAL TEXTS

Data Protection Directive: Directive 95/46/EC of the European Parliament and of the Council of 24 October 1995 on the protection of individuals with regard to the processing of personal data and on the free movement of such data, OJ L 281 (1995), https://eur-lex.europa.eu/legal-content/EN/TXT/?uri=celex%3A31995L0046.

ePrivacy Directive: Directive 2009/136/EC of the European Parliament and of the Council of 25 November 2009 amending Directive 2002/22/EC on universal service and users' rights relating to electronic communications networks and services, Directive 2002/58/EC concerning the processing of personal data and the protection of privacy in the electronic communications sector and Regulation (EC) No 2006/2004 on co-operation between national authorities responsible for the enforcement of consumer protection laws, OJ L 337 (2009), https://eur-lex.europa.eu/legal-content/EN/TXT/?uri=celex%3A32009L0136.

EU Charter: Charter of Fundamental Rights of the European Union, OJ C 326 (2012), https://eur-lex.europa.eu/legal-content/EN/TXT/?uri=celex:C2012/326/02.

GDPR: Regulation (EU) 2016/679 of the European Parliament and of the Council of 27 April 2016 on the protection of natural persons with regard to the processing of personal data and on the free movement of such data, and repealing Directive 95/46/EC (General Data Protection Regulation) (Text with EEA relevance), OJ L 119 (2016), https://eur-lex.europa.eu/legal-content/EN/TXT/?uri=celex%3A32016R0679.

HIPPA: Health Insurance Portability and Accountability Act (1996), https://aspe.hhs.gov/report/health-insurance-portability-and-accountability-act-1996 (relevant to the US market).

NIS Directive: Directive (EU) 2016/1148 of the European Parliament and of the Council of 6 July 2016 concerning measures for a high common level of security of network and information systems across the Union, OJ L 194 (2016), https://eur-lex.europa.eu/eli/dir/2016/1148/oj.

OECD guidelines: OECD Guidelines on the Protection of Privacy and Transborder Flows of Personal Data (1980), www.oecd.org/internet/ieconomy/oecdguidelinesonthe protectionofprivacyandtransborderflowsofpersonaldata.htm.

PsD2: Directive (EU) 2015/2366 of the European Parliament and of the Council of 25 November 2015 on payment services in the internal market, amending Directives 2002/65/EC, 2009/110/EC and 2013/36/EU and Regulation (EU) No 1093/2010, and repealing Directive 2007/64/EC, OJ L 337 (2015), https://eur-lex.europa.eu/legal-content/EN/TXT/?uri=CELEX:32015L2366.

OTHER ONLINE RESOURCES

Information on the GDPR and other legislation

Children Online: https://www.twobirds.com/en/in-focus/general-data-protection-regulation/gdpr-tracker/children (list of age requirements by country)

DLA Piper Data Protection Laws of the World: https://www.dlapiperdataprotection.com (a user-friendly free compilation of data protection laws globally)

ENISA: https://www.enisa.europa.eu (EU's cyber security agency, developing cyber security standards, frameworks, recommendations – a free resource)

GDPR Enforcement Tracker: https://www.enforcementtracker.com (list of GDPR sanctions)

GDPR Tracker: https://www.twobirds.com/en/in-focus/general-data-protection-regulation/gdpr-tracker (details of country-specific legislation that supplements the GDPR)

Generally Accepted Privacy Principles (GAPP): https://www.cpacanada.ca/-/media/site/operational/ms-member-services/docs/00250-generally-accepted-privacy-principles.pdf?la=en&hash=284D936484F7D77307F80A9951E015D551B62DBC (10 privacy principles that can be used to create a global data protection compliance programme, developed by the American Institute of Certified Public Accountants (AICPA) and Chartered Professional Accountants Canada (CPCA))

International Organization for Standardization (ISO): https://www.iso.org/home.html (the global standards' institute, publishing various global standards with relevance for information security, risk management, auditing, privacy-enhancing technologies, privacy management etc.)

List of EU member states' derogations: https://iapp.org/resources/tools/eu-member-state-gdpr-derogation-implementation (only accessible for members of the IAPP)

Privacy Maturity Model: https://www.cpacanada.ca/en/business-and-accounting-resources/other-general-business-topics/information-management-and-technology/publications/business-and-organizational-privacy-policy-resources/measuring-a-privacy-program (the global framework for managing a data protection compliance programme and measuring privacy risks developed by AICPA and CPCA)

Analysis

AICPA (American Institute of CPAs): https://www.aicpa.org (the American Institute of Certified Public Accountants whom among other things have developed the GAPP and Privacy Maturity Model)

Centre for Information Policy Leadership: https://www.informationpolicycentre.com/cipl-white-papers.html (a resource of well-thought-out legal analysis on data protection)

Chronicle of Data Protection: https://www.hoganlovells.com/en/hldataprotection (legal analysis for legal experts by Hogan Lovells)

CIO from IDG: https://www.cio.com/ (global media site with news and analysis for the CIO and business managers by IDG)

Computer World by IDG: https://www.computerworld.com/ (global media site with news and analysis for the tech savvy and business managers by IDG)

CPCA (Chartered Professional Accountants Canada): https://www.cpacanada.ca (Canadian Institute of Chartered Accountants whom among other things have developed the GAPP and Privacy Maturity Model)

DataGuidance by OneTrust: https://www.dataguidance.com (a platform consisting of up-to-date, comprehensive, global data protection law tables arranged in various ways – for example, by country or by topic, with daily updates, news alerts and data protection analysis; it is supported by both in-house data protection experts at privacy technology supplier OneTrust and leading data protection law firms)

GDPR Summary: https://www.gdprsummary.com (data protection blog on privacy, ePrivacy and the GDPR for generalists and business managers with legal analysis, guidance and checklists on GDPR's impact on business)

Privacy, Security and Information Law: https://privacylawblog.fieldfisher.com (legal analysis blog for legal experts by Fieldfisher)

PSBE Cyber News: https://www.cybernewsgroup.co.uk/all-news/ (cybersecurity blog with global focus)

Legal newsletters

Data Protection Report: https://www.dataprotectionreport.com (by law firm Norton Rose Fulbright)

IAPP Daily Dashboard: https://iapp.org/news/daily-dashboard (daily newsletter for the most important privacy and data protection news from around the world; free resource)

Privacy & Information Security Law Blog: https://www.huntonprivacyblog.com (by law firm Hunton Andrews Kurth)

NOTABLE PROFESSIONAL CONFERENCES ON PRIVACY AND SECURITY

IAPP Data Protection Intensive: https://iapp.org/conferences (intensive training opportunities held in various cities)

IAPP Europe Data Protection Congress: https://iapp.org/conference/iapp-europe-data-protection-congress (European focus; features the top names in data protection from respected privacy activists to government officials to senior management in the tech industry)

IAPP Global Privacy Summit: https://iapp.org/conference/global-privacy-summit (global focus with comprehensive agenda; features the top names in data protection from respected privacy activists to government officials to senior management in the tech industry)

Nordic Privacy Arena: https://dpforum.se/nordic-privacy-arena (annual Nordic conference on the trending privacy topics)

EDUCATION AND ACCREDITATION

BCS, The Chartered Institute for IT: https://www.bcs.org/get-qualified/certifications-for-professionals/gdpr-and-data-protection-certifications (foundation and practitioner certificates in data protection)

IAPP (International Association of Privacy Professionals): https://iapp.org (various training courses, seminars and certifications such as the CIPP-X certifications)

ISACA Certified Data Privacy Solutions Engineer: https://www.isaca.org/credentialing/certified-data-privacy-solutions-engineer (an international professional association focused on IT governance that publishes and certifies IT security standards)

Various organisations offer the following qualifications (issued by the IAPP):

CIPP Certification (EU and US laws and regulations)

CIPP/M (operational qualification)

CIPP/T (technical qualification)

CODES OF CONDUCT

According to the GDPR, associations and other bodies representing categories of controllers or processors should be encouraged to draw up codes of conduct and have them validated by the competent data protection authorities. The following is the only one that we are aware of that has been certified.

EU Cloud Code of Conduct (CoC): https://eucoc.cloud/en/ home.html (A code of conduct for cloud service providers validated according to Article 28(5) of the GDPR. The code was developed by the Cloud Select Industry Group, convened by the European Commission with the involvement and advice of the Directorate-General for Justice. Development of the code was further informed by input from the Article 29 Working Party.)

INDEX

CPSIA information can be obtained
at www.ICGtesting.com
Printed in the USA
LVHW050246280122
709355LV00015B/1646

9 781780 174365